How To Turn That First Glance Into A Date

Suzanne J. Price

www.suzanneprice.com

SJP

Coaching & Consulting

Suzanne J. Price

www.suzanneprice.com

How To Turn That First Glance Into A Date

Copyright © 2009 by Suzanne J. Price

Canadian Intellectual Property Certificate of Registration 2009

Published by Suzanne J. Price

All rights reserved. No part of this book may be used or reproduced in any manner whatsoever without prior written consent of the author.

ISBN   978-0-9812862-0-4

Dedicated To You

This book is dedicated to every man and woman who, by hesitating and not approaching an attractive stranger, or anyone for that matter who you have found attractive, suffered the consequences of a regretful "Missed Connection".

I also dedicate it to anyone who has a Secret Crush on someone who you adore, but you just haven't been able to bring yourself to let him or her know how you feel, yet.

And to those of you who, through stubbornness, misunderstandings or events out of your control, parted ways with the person who just might be the true love of your life.

And finally, to all of the single men and women around the world who are looking to find that one special person that would make your life complete.

I wish you love

Suzanne

www.suzanneprice.com

www.giveromancea2ndchance.com

www.realrelationshiprevolution.com

Part One
Overcome The Fear Of Rejection

Chapter 1   **Page 13**

Ah, That First Glance!

Chapter 2   **Page 17**

So What Are You Afraid Of Anyway?

Chapter 3   **Page 33**

How The Fear Of Rejection Can Develop

Chapter 4   **Page 43**

How To Overcome The Fear Of Rejection

Part Two

Become A More Confident Version Of Yourself

Chapter 5   **Page 65**

Reinventing Yourself – Creating A New And More Confident You!

Chapter 6   **Page 87**

Developing The Habits Of A Confident Person

Chapter 7   **Page 103**

The Secrets To Becoming A Super Attractive Person

Chapter 8   **Page 115**

You May Never Get A Second Chance At Love At First Sight

Chapter 9   **Page 139**

How To Use Your Body Language To Build Rapport

Chapter 10   **Page 155**

To Become A Fun Loving Dynamic Free

Spirit You Need To Flirt

Chapter 11   **Page 185**

Say What You Mean And Mean What You Say

Chapter 12   **Page 205**

How To Turn That First Glance Into A Date

Introduction

How To Turn That First Glance Into A Date was written to help the reader overcome the fear of rejection and develop the confidence to approach, talk to, flirt with and ask someone out on a date, *in real life!*

Using NLP, coaching and fear busting exercises, this book offers a step by step approach to first help you overcome the fear of rejection, and then develop the confidence necessary to make those regretful missed connections, a thing of the past.

Part One

Overcome The Fear Of Rejection

Chapter 1

Ah, That First Glance!

Ah, that first glance! You know the one where you look up and see a beautiful stranger. You feel an instant attraction, but wonder what to do. You can only imagine how great it would be to have someone like that in your life, and you feel the urge to approach.

Hesitating to contemplate your move, your eyes suddenly meet but you look away quickly as if to pretend that you never even noticed the object of your desire. Asking yourself "What *did* I do that for?" a familiar little voice pops into your head telling you what an idiot you are.

Realizing it's now or never you desperately want to strike up a conversation and the pressure is on. As you try to muster up the confidence, you become painfully aware of that seemingly invisible force that has held you back so many times before.

Luckily, your natural instinct tells you to take another look, after all, that's what happens when two people feel an initial attraction, but that negative little voice pipes up again, yelling "don't do it, they will see you and then what will you do?"

Your mind starts racing, bombarding you with negative scenarios that undermine you, and before you know it your little fantasy has been hijacked by all of those self defeating thoughts which pop into your head whenever you're around someone that you find attractive.

Determined to take action you wonder what to do. Smile? Talk? Or, just leave the scene and rationalize why they couldn't possibly be interested in you anyway!

So you come up with what seems to be the most rational answer, talking! That seems to be a good idea, but what should you say? What if you say the wrong thing or worse yet, what if you fumble your words?

You can't resist any longer, so you glance back over and ... Oh Gawd, the worst possible scenario.... They're looking back at you too....you've been busted!

Hmm, now what? You can feel yourself blushing, or is that a full blown panic attack? Never mind, by looking away again and deliberately ignoring the object of your desire you've probably just sent your beautiful stranger the message that you are not interested anyway. Then before you take the chance to seize your golden opportunity, your adored subject turns around and walks right back out of your life. And perhaps the worst thing about this whole scenario is that, the fact they also glanced back at you probably meant that they found *you* attractive *too*.

If that's not bad enough, you spend the next two weeks (or two years) beating yourself up for letting yourself down. Now, feeling like such a coward, it probably feels as though you have had an evil curse put upon you which has always prevented you from connecting with anyone that you have ever found attractive in the past. And as you wonder if you will ever get the chance to bump into your perfect stranger again you get that familiar sinking feeling in your gut because you seriously doubt that you will ever have the confidence to approach them anyway.

Sound familiar? Of course it does, because what I just described has to be one of the most common *coulda, shoulda, woulda* blunders that we have all experienced when in the presence of an attractive stranger. Or for that matter anyone who we feel attracted to but just cannot bring ourselves to let our intentions be known. So many missed opportunities! So many disappointments! But that is all about to change.

The good news is that your past is not your destiny. So if you are ready to learn **How To Turn That Next First Glance Into A Date**, then I would love to help. You do have the power to put an end to disappointing missed connections, and the potential to change future outcomes of chance encounters with attractive strangers. So with a little coaching, accompanied with some great tips, tools and the right knowledge, you will soon develop the skills and confidence to approach, start a conversation with, and ask anyone out. You will soon have the confidence, ***To Turn That Next First Glance Into A Date.***

If you have had a similar experience to the one described above or would like to connect with a long lost love or someone who you let slip away, I invite you to visit www.giveromancea2ndchance.com

Chapter 2

So What Are You Afraid Of Anyway?

As you are kicking and berating yourself for not being able to do something as simple as talk to someone you find attractive, you might also be driving yourself crazy wondering *why*? Why is this so difficult? How come I don't know what to do? Why am I so nervous when I want to approach someone who I am attracted to?

All these questions with perhaps one simple answer! No matter how you try to rationalize your fears, the underlying reason for your hesitations, apprehensions or whatever you want to call your experience is, ***the fear of rejection***, and the feelings of shame or embarrassment that accompany it.

Rejection is a de-motivator. The fear of being rejected by another person or group can prevent us from motivating ourselves towards success or achievement in any area of our life. If we fear being rejected in social groups or business settings these fears of rejection may hinder us from developing relationships in any sort of social or business situation. When the fear of rejection is this widespread it has the capability to negatively impact us in any area where we need or want social acceptance. This may include friendship or any professional relationship.

If on the other hand we suffer from a fear of approaching an attractive stranger, or for that matter any person that we find attractive but cannot bring ourselves to approach and let our feelings or intentions be known, this will certainly negatively impact our personal and romantic relationships.

Everyone at some point in their life has experienced rejection. In fact it would be almost impossible to find a single man, woman or child on this planet who has never encountered this negative experience. The fear of rejection can be the result of something that someone has actually said or done to us, or by how they responded to us. It could have been that we felt rejected by the way someone simply looked at us, or because of the body language they used when they were around us. On the other hand we may actually create our own internal feelings of rejection by what we think or how we feel about ourselves.

At this point it is not important to know when or where you personally developed this fear. Although it is likely that you can still recall some particular situations where you have experienced rejection in the past, it is not necessarily those past experiences that still hold you back in present time, nor will it be in future similar situations. The sad truth is that very often your present fear of rejection will be a result of your own self doubt, and without realizing it, you may actually be the very person who is rejecting yourself. If this is true for you, then you could end up becoming your own worst enemy.

Perhaps the most important thing to remember is that no matter where we developed our response to rejection, it is how we respond to an event that will ultimately determine our level of motivation to either approach or retreat from a similar situation in the future. So, one of the things that I want to show you in the following chapters is how we can turn our fears around and change how we react to our feelings and beliefs about our past negative experiences, or perceived future threats of rejection.

By doing so we can remove this de-motivator which has in the past sabotaged us from achieving our greatest goals and desires. This process will leave us with the freedom and confidence to reach for our dreams and desires and approach and interact with people who we would love to have in our lives.

Now my question to you is this: Are you ready to trade in your fear of rejection for the freedom and confidence ***To Turn That Next First Glance Into A Date?***

Dispelling Some Old Beliefs About Rejection

There could be any number of reasons why you have developed a fear of rejection, but there is a good chance that your apprehensions and nervousness have their roots firmly planted in one or more of the following issues:

- ♥ You have experienced a nasty case of rejection when approaching an attractive person, or someone that you have admired in the past.

- ♥ You witnessed someone else experiencing rejection and it affected you so negatively that you have become a bit gun shy when asking for something you want from another person. Such as to be accepted, or perhaps a date.

- ♥ Unconsciously, you practice negative mind reading and you anticipate the worst possible negative responses from the people you would like to approach and ask out.

- ♥ You lack confidence in yourself either in general, your appearance, or your social and dating skills, so you think that you are just not good enough.

- ♥ Your lack of experience in dating or being in a relationship makes it difficult to start the process of approaching an attractive stranger for fear of what to do next.

- ♥ You are a very shy person and find talking to strangers to be very stressful in any situation.

Addressing any or all of these issues and practicing the exercises in this book will help you become more confident in yourself. This will allow you to start to build a good foundation for a stronger self esteem, and in turn you will notice that you are having a lot more fun in the world of dating. Now let's take a look at some ways you might conquer these obstacles.

- ♥ **You have experienced a nasty case of rejection when approaching an attractive person, or someone that you admired in the past.**

Rejection is something that most of us will avoid at all costs. However, this is not always possible, leaving most of us with at least one unfavourable memory of a time when we felt rejected by someone we were attracted to in the past.

The experience of being turned down or rejected by someone that you are very fond of or attracted to is probably one of the worst forms of rejection that anyone could possibly encounter. When we put ourselves out there to present ourselves to someone in the hopes of becoming a potential partner, we are at our most vulnerable. If that person turns us down, it may seem as if they are rejecting us based on our physical being or our personality. We may interpret this to mean that we just didn't measure up to what the other person finds attractive, and may internalize this rejection to mean, *I'm just not good enough* or *I'm not an attractive enough person.*

Such past rejections can and often do act as negative anchors that discourage us from taking action in similar future situations. Partly because of the disappointment that our feelings are not going to be reciprocated, and partly because of the possible embarrassment or humiliation that accompanied the event, we would more than likely take this rejection very personally as it would be associated with our identity. The more personal the experience of being rejected, the stronger the effect it will likely have over us in future similar events.

In contrast a situation where rejection might not seem so personal may be if we had applied for a job but didn't get it. This event, although disappointing probably wouldn't have such a negative impact on our ego since it would seem far more likely that we were being judged on our ability to do the job and not on who we are.

Therefore, we may look at this scenario as if we were being rejected based on our capabilities, and not our identity, which often seems to be the way we interpret things when it comes to getting involved in a personal relationship.

Perhaps the most important thing to be aware of here is that our experiences are ultimately all about perception. If we interpret rejection as a personal attack every time we get turned down, our beliefs can end up sabotaging us from getting anything or anyone we desire.

- **You witnessed someone else experiencing rejection, and it affected you so negatively that you have become a bit gun shy when asking for something that you want from another person. Such as to be accepted, or perhaps a date.**

Rejection seems to be transferable from one person to another, meaning that if we witness someone else being rejected we may unconsciously use that experience to rationalize and justify our own fears.

Whenever we see someone else getting hurt in some way, perhaps by being rejected, we may feel some empathy for them and in turn experience some level of their emotional pain. If the emotions that were triggered at the time we witnessed the event were intense enough, then that external experience may also become part of our own reality and compound our fear of rejection even more.

The more often we see or hear about these events taking place, the more our own thoughts, feelings and beliefs about rejection may be reinforced. These experiences can actually affect us in the same way as if the event had happened to us personally.

Another circumstance that can validate any anchors to rejection may be when we experience rejection in other parts of our life. These situations may have nothing to do with personal relationships, but the associated thoughts and feelings of rejection, shame or embarrassment from other situations can permeate throughout our lives and can become anchored to similar situations. This again can reinforce our feelings, beliefs and personal experience of what rejection means to us.

The negative anchors which have now been created by these associated experiences may then automatically be elicited whenever we experience any event that has the potential to bring about the feelings of shame, embarrassment or rejection.

Although I cannot guarantee that you will never encounter rejection again, I can assure you that you have the power to change how any experience of rejection will affect you in the future.

- ♥ **Unconsciously, you practice negative mind reading and you anticipate the worst possible negative responses from the people you would like to approach and ask out.**

As if the actual experience of being rejected isn't bad enough, some of us even reject ourselves before we allow others the privilege first. If this is true for you then you are probably your own worst enemy. One of the ways that we do this is when we see someone that we really like, but instead of making a connection, flirting a little and perhaps striking up a conversation, we instead assume that they won't like us then act in a way that would give them the impression that we are not interested anyway. By doing this we are literally rejecting ourselves first, and in turn rejecting that other person in the same process.

Mind reading is a huge obstacle for so many people who literally freeze when in the presence of an attractive stranger. We do this by anticipating some sort of negative outcome of what might happen if we do approach the person we are attracted to. If you are always conscious of this negative anticipation it may even prevent you from making initial eye contact, smiling or just acknowledging the other person's presence.

At this level of avoidance the only message that you are giving off is that you are not in the least bit interested. In order to motivate yourself to take that first step towards making a connection you first need to stop the mind reading and anticipating the possibility of receiving a negative response, and then you need to take a realistic look at what the reality of the situation may actually be.

For instance, when you want to approach someone that you find attractive, since you probably won't know anything about him/her including their marital status, their confidence level, or what is going on in their life at that moment in time, I think we can safely say that there is at least a fifty percent chance that things could actually go quite well. However, if things don't go quite as planned you have to consider the following.

Now with a very realistic starting point of 50/50, if you do get turned down the next time you approach someone that you are attracted to just remember that the reason probably has absolutely nothing to do with you at all. The object of your desire may simply be having a bad day or it may be a case of bad timing. Or, on the other hand they may be so nervous and taken off guard by your interest that they might act aloof out of fear. This probably sounds very self sabotaging, but it is much more common than you might think. We women beat ourselves up over this one a lot.

Then, there is always a chance that he or she is actually married or in a committed relationship or taking time out from dating to focus on other things. So as you can see there are so many reasons why someone might not respond favourably to you and their opinion of you might not even come into the equation.

Feeling that you might not measure up to the other person's standards is just a form of perhaps very inaccurate mind reading or self rejection. And, if you are going to go around rejecting yourself every time you meet someone who you find attractive, I would strongly suggest that you work with a coach such as myself who can help you to build confidence and make yourself as marketable as possible. Otherwise you could be setting yourself up for a potentially nerve wracking experience every time you want to approach someone who you find attractive.

The truth is most people would be flattered just knowing that you fancied them enough to approach no matter how nervous or shy you are. And even if your approach doesn't lead to anything more than a pleasant and friendly acknowledgment of each other's presence, at least you are putting yourself out there to practice and build confidence so that you will feel ready the next time someone great comes along.

- ♥ **You lack confidence in yourself either in general, your appearance, or your social and dating skills, so you think that you are just not good enough.**

Most people at some point in their life will experience insecurities that can cause them to become nervous when meeting someone new, dating or courting a new relationship. Often we feel this way because we are afraid that we are not going to meet the other person's expectations, so we doubt ourselves in some part of our life. Although our self doubt may be very specific it will very often revolve around issues such as our personal image and appearance, our self confidence, or our social skills and ability to relate to this new person. However, when it comes to relationships our insecurities may have more to do with what we feel that we have to offer in order to entice this person into our life, and keep them interested enough to commit.

These insecurities can cause us to feel very vulnerable and stir up underlying fears of being rejected, or worse yet abandoned if this person finds out who we truly are. Perhaps the only thing worse than this is if we feel that we have no choice in the matter and that we are unable to change ourselves or our situation. But, thankfully this type of belief couldn't be any further from the truth.

To develop true confidence throughout life you need to develop the attitude that you can, and maybe should always strive to be the best version of yourself possible, in whatever area of life that may be. And that you should always be open and willing to reinvent yourself and bring about change.

Perhaps, the only reason that you have not become the person that you want to be is because you have not had the awareness or tools necessary in order to achieve this until now. The importance of knowing what you want is paramount, because without knowing this it would be very difficult for you to either believe what is possible or commit to the goal.

Change can and will happen as long as you know what you want and how you are going to get it, but for many people the process of finding this clarity and awareness is the hardest part. If you need help finding clarity you can download The Triple AAA Coaching Tool on www.suzanneprice.com. By realizing that anything is possible, and by taking the action necessary to get to where you want to be, you are empowering yourself every step of the way.

As you start the process of reinventing yourself it is important to realize that you need to set out both long and short term goals and realize that although it is possible to see immediate change in some parts of your life, other change may take longer before you see the benefits. Also keep those goals in focus at all times, I like to do this be revisiting them every morning, usually before I even get out of bed, when I also think about and plan which of those goals I can actually achieve that day. Then you need to take action.

Confidence is something that can develop, image is something that can be changed, and skills can be learnt. With a clear awareness, a little determination, the commitment to succeed and some great tips found in this book you will be able to start to take the necessary action to achieve, and become anything that you want in life.

There is a great article on my coaching website called, Why Clearly Defined Goals And Positive Thinking Don't Necessarily Work. There you will also find some worksheets which will help you to start creating the awareness of who and what you want to become in your life.

- **♥ Your lack of experience in dating or being in a relationship makes it difficult to start the process of approaching an attractive stranger for fear of what to do next.**

Relationships can and often do take on a life of their own. When you have made the connection with someone great you just have to wing it and go with the flow. When in a relationship there should be no set rules, and no right or wrong ways to do things. A good relationship should simply be two people interacting and responding to each other's words, gestures, body language and energy, and there should be a natural flow.

If you find that you meet someone who has a lot more experience at dating or being in a relationship than you do, the chances are that they won't even notice your inexperience. And if they do they will probably love the fact that they can lead the way as it can often be less of a battle. Don't be discouraged by your inexperience as this should mean that you have more to look forward to and be excited about.

- **♥ You are a very shy person and find talking to strangers to be very stressful in any situation.**

If you are a naturally shy person and find that social events or dating cause you a great deal of anxiety so you avoid these situations all together only to then feel lonely and disappointed, you are probably missing out on the very things that could really enrich your life. This may seem like a hopeless and desperate situation but there is hope. However, it may mean that you have to step out of your comfort zone first.

Start by practicing some of the fear busting exercises that you will learn in the following chapters. Then sign up for a public speaking course and some dance lessons. Taking a course in public speaking will train you in a safe environment to speak up in front of people. And, since most of them would be feeling the same way as you are, you will probably find the participants to be very supportive of each other.

Dancing is another great way to build your confidence and overcome your fear while having fun at the same time. When dancing you are moving your body and releasing your spirit and it is a very social thing to do. It is a fantastic way to interact with others, especially with those of the opposite sex. Also, most of the people in a dance class will be at the same level as you, and everyone will be in the same boat together.

When you are looking for dance lessons, find out if the dancing is partner dancing. If so and you don't have a partner, check with the instructor to see if they make the partners revolve around the room. This is a very common practice in dance lessons as it gives everyone the opportunity to dance with different partners.

There are great dance lessons offered in most community centers but also check out some private dance schools. I have found that a lot of them will put on a dance or offer dance practice time after the class. This is a great opportunity to reconnect with people that you have just met in the lesson and the expectation to partner up to dance has already been set, so there is less chance of getting turned down. It is often this dance time where you will get the opportunity to get to know each other and build great rapport.

Just go out, have fun, get some exercise, move your body and set your spirit free, and meet some great people at the same time. And remember, nobody will ever guess that you are actually there to practice your social skills as well as learn to dance.

Chapter 3

How The Fear Of Rejection Can Develop

Many ancient therapies teach us that anything that has ever happened to us from the moment we were born, or possibly conceived, is stored in our body and our nervous system. These experiences may be either positive or negative and will inevitably produce an emotional response. If the emotional response is strong enough, there is a very good chance that our experience could develop into a future unconscious trigger or anchor. These anchors later determine how we will respond to, and experience similar future events throughout our lives.

The fear of rejection or the feeling of being rejected is a very good example of a negative experience and response. As we go through life, even if we don't actually remember those earliest experiences which may have originally caused us to feel the negative emotions associated with being rejected, whenever we find ourselves in a similar situation the anchor may be triggered.

This in turn will cause us to once again re-experience the negative emotions which we now know to be associated with any form of rejection. Every time we experience one of these events, it reinforces the trigger and can make the negative emotional response even stronger. This pattern over time becomes part of our programming and contributes to who we become, what we believe about ourselves in any particular situation, and how we respond to these events.

Depending on how intense our fear of rejection is, it may also be considered a phobia. Fears and phobias are created in exactly the same way, and that is with the help of our own imagination.

Usually we develop a fear unconsciously as it is often a learned response. Since our brain doesn't necessarily differentiate between what is real and what is imagined it leaves us to develop fears from various different situations. In fact our fears can become even more exaggerated by an event that we didn't even personally experience ourselves. We may simply see or hear about a situation where someone is being or has been rejected, then by internalizing that external experience we allow it to confirm our own beliefs and fears, and it eventually becomes part of our own reality.

To prove my point, consider the following examples. Most people who have a fear of snakes have never actually seen or been near one in real life. And many children who are afraid of dogs quite likely learned this response from a parent. If that is not enough to convince you, consider this, thousands of people developed a fear or phobia of water after watching the movie Jaws. For some this phobia is so intense and debilitating that they can no longer even wash their hands, take a shower, or step outside when it is raining. Knowing this, you have to ask yourself this question: was their experience actually real or was it imagined?

Sometimes the event was actually imagined, but unfortunately the brain does not always know the difference between what is real and what is imagined. So with this image in your mind which may also include sounds or any input from any of our senses, we continue to develop that fear and perhaps even create our own phobias. This is a process which can be powered up by creating pictures in our minds and then reinforcing them by adding associated negative thoughts.

The repetition of thinking about, or visualizing something may seem as if it is happening over and over again and the fear continues to grow stronger, and so do the negative emotions that have become attached to it. Then whenever we think about the situation, thing, or event that originally caused us these feelings, it is likely that we trigger these negative emotions again and reinforce the fear. This is how any fear can literally spiral out of control.

Here is a simplistic explanation of how a fear develops and manifests into physical symptoms in the body – First imagine water running through a hose pipe which develops a kink in it. What happens? The water flow is cut off and can no longer run through the hose. The fear response in the body is much the same. We have life energy flowing through our body on a continuous basis. When we encounter a fear or negative emotional situation, such as being rejected, it is as if there is a disruption or a block in the energy flow, just like the kink in the hose pipe.

When you experience an energy disruption, your energy force plummets and depending on the intensity of the fear, your physical energy can drop by up to 80% - (you might recall watching a movie where someone was being told about a tragic event and the bearer of the bad news would say "you might want to sit down, I have some bad news"). Also, your brain hemispheres lose communication with each other – (ever wonder why you can't think straight while in a stressful situation, such as wanting to talk to an attractive person?) And the "fight or flight" response may kick in, and in the case of wanting to approach someone you find attractive, you might instead retreat or simply avoid eye contact.

This all sounds very interesting, but what has it got to do with for instance, a fear of rejection that causes you to avoid approaching someone that you find attractive?

Now consider the following examples of how a specific fear is developed.

Imagine you are driving along in your car and all of a sudden someone comes speeding out of a side street and crashes into you. Your body will probably experience quite a severe stress response and lock in any physical or emotional pain that was incurred at that exact moment in time. This may include anything you felt, saw, heard, smelled, tasted or imagined at that very moment in time, and the time revolving around the event. It is at this time that your energy system would also experience an energy disruption that would cause, let's say a bubble, in the energy system. It is as if this experience is now all melded together and has created a fear response in your mind/body system. The "bubble" will remain there until it is released.

Now it is quite likely that from this time on every time you drive past that same intersection you will think about the accident, and you may even feel at the very least some apprehension. You might even experience some of the same symptoms or reactions you had at the time of the accident, and you may even feel this response at every intersection you drive through.

You now have a new fear locked into your subconscious mind and body. Your mind/body will have developed quite a strong anchor to fear around driving through intersections and in turn triggers the mind/body response whenever you are in that situation. If the initial response was intense enough this fear could permeate into circumstances associated with the accident and cause you to become fearful of driving in general, or for some, even fearful of getting into a car.

So how does this work in developing a fear of rejection?

Developing a fear of rejection happens in very much the same way. As a child you may have been teased or taunted about anything from the way you walked to the way you looked, to where your parents came from or where your Dad worked. Or, people might have poked fun at your name. No matter what the situation was, it is very likely that it bothered you in some way and at some level eroded away at your self esteem. Even if it was just a little bit, it all counts.

Or you may have had to stand up in class to spell something or read out loud and you fumbled your words and everyone laughed at you. This scenario has been the making of many a fear of public speaking, or even a fear of speaking up in general, including talking to an attractive stranger.

Or, your fear may have started from a time when you tried your absolute best to get good grades and didn't do quite as you hoped, so not only did you beat yourself up, but you also felt like you had disappointed your parents. And your friends poked fun at you again. You can add that to the pile of injuries to your self-esteem. So already you are very aware of what it feels like to be embarrassed or poked fun of and you haven't even reached the dating stage of your life yet.

Then the big day comes when you have that first crush on someone and you get teased and harassed by family and friends, which just goes to prove that you should have done a better job at keeping it a secret. Bingo!... a secret, isn't that what we do when we find someone that we like, we keep it a secret, *from them*!

Anyway, you take a deep breath and forge ahead to attempt to talk to your secret crush only to have them laugh in your face and run off to tell all of their friends that you like them. And truth be known they probably acted that way just because they were scared anyway, but not knowing this you assume the worst. Hmmm.... Now we can see where these fears may have started, and the possibilities could have been endless. And, in the process of all of these emotional injures and attacks on your self esteem, your mind and body goes through very much the same reaction, and process, although at varying levels of intensity, to how your fear was created in the car accident scenario.

Then we grow up and talk with friends about getting a boyfriend or girlfriend (whatever the case may be), and we share in and hear about other people's horror stories of the good, the bad and the ugly situations that people encounter when approaching someone they like. This all confirms our negative beliefs and fears of all the bad things that might happen if you approach your attractive stranger, or anyone else for that matter who you find attractive. This compounds our fears even more and the cycle goes on. Need I say more?

However, there is good news, and that is that you do not have to carry around all of these old hurts and anchors that make you feel bad and cause you to act in ways that no longer serve you. I will show you how you can change these patterns as you read through the next few chapters.

The point is that it doesn't matter where or how we develop our fears, they can eventually became the glitch in our mind/body system, which, whenever revisited, can elicit the same old feelings that continue to hold us back. But with the help of the exercises in this book you can learn to override the details and get straight to releasing the negative emotional blocks, which in turn will also release the stress from your mind/body system, that bubble that I had mentioned before. By doing so you will no longer experience the negative anchors whenever you find yourself with an opportunity *To Turn That First Glance Into A Date.*

So, I invite you to take advantage of what you learn in this book and use it to your best benefit. The exercises in the following chapters are set out in a way as to build upon each other, so I'm sure that if you follow the program from start to finish, you will be amazed at how you too can overcome the fears that have until now held you back. You can apply these exercises to any area of your life, but especially practice them to help you overcome the fears and obstacles that get in the way of your dating experiences and social interactions.

Chapter 4

How To Overcome The Fear Of Rejection

Many of us carry our fears around with us throughout our lives, perhaps without even realizing how much control they have over us. Fears can and often do prevent us from getting whatever we truly want, meaning at best, we will often find ourselves settling for "second best".

Part of the reason that we allow these fears to have so much control over us is because we are not always necessarily aware of exactly what it is that we are afraid of. And even if we are, if our fear is strong enough it will probably do a good job of protecting us from whatever the true fear is, in a twisted kind of way.

When we have a fear its purpose may very well be to prevent us from confronting that which we are actually afraid of. For instance, if a person says that he or she wished that they didn't have the fear, but then avoided doing whatever is needed in order to get rid of it, then perhaps the benefits of having such a fear may seem to outweigh the prospects of not having it at all.

A good example of this would be if a person is afraid of flying and the fear or phobia prevents him or her from getting on a plane. But if that person was to give up that fear it could be even scarier as they would no longer have an excuse not to get on that plane anymore. It may sound silly but it is a very common scenario. When this happens it may not be the actual fear which is causing the problem, but instead a belief that the person has developed about him or herself, and their identity which revolves around that particular fear.

Another reason that we suffer throughout our lives with these fears may be because we think that the fear is simply a part of who we are, as if it is some part of our genetic makeup. But this is not necessarily true. And because of these reasons I believe that if you truly want to overcome a fear or phobia, you first need to deal with the actual fear, and then you need to create a new identity around this particular issue.

Also, many of us may feel that we are stuck with our fears because we may simply not be aware of the options that could help us to overcome them. And, if this is the case, we would probably also be unaware of just how easy it can be to rid ourselves of these fears. The exercises I use for dealing with fears do not go into the history and gory details as to how the fear was created. Instead, I use a very forward-focused approach which I would like to share with you in this chapter.

The following exercises are laid out in a specific order with each exercise building upon the previous one. If you feel that you have a very ingrained or intense fear around dating, or approaching or talking to someone who you are attracted to, I do offer online as well as one-on-one coaching.

Please Read Before You Attempt The Following Exercises.

Even though I have personally used these exercises with great success and have seen and heard of amazing outcomes, you must understand that I am not a doctor nor do I work in a medical or mental health profession. I work as a coach in the area of personal development. Therefore, if you choose to do these exercises, you must do so at your own discretion. I am in no way advocating that you use these exercises to attempt to overcome any sort of emotional or mental disorder, and if you have any concern for yourself or others with regard to such issues, you should seek advice from a doctor or professional mental health specialist.

A Little Bit About The Modalities I Like To Work With And Why I Use Them.

I work with exercises derived from NLP, TFT, EFT, TFH, One Brain Learning Awareness, and Tapping Into Your Mind Body Magic. I do so because they are the most powerful processes I have ever encountered and I can personally vouch for them as my first experience using them was to overcome some fears and phobias of my own.

Like many people, in my younger days I did a great job at avoiding a lot of things that made me anxious. The problem with this is that I missed out on some great opportunities, and in the process reinforced a lot of avoidance behaviours. This behaviour in itself caused its own problems because I often found myself feeling let down and very disappointed.

There were so many things I wanted to do, but I often didn't follow through, and I avoided some great opportunities for fear of being fearful and anxious. In doing so I was constantly letting myself down, much like we do when we don't date or won't ask someone out. My avoidance and disappointment eventually developed into panic attacks and anxiety severe enough that I reached a point where I was merely existing but not really living my life. An extreme case but my point is about the exercises.

It was at this time that I went in search of something to help me overcome my fears so I could really start to live my life and enjoy everything I had been missing out on. I wanted to be unstoppable! And it was during this search that I came across NLP, TFT, EFT TFH and One Brain. These modalities proved to be so powerful that I decided to train in them myself, first to overcome my own fears so that I could live my life to the fullest, and also to help others overcome their fears too.

Because of my own experience I can truly vouch for these methods and I have used and continue to use them for myself, and my clients to help alleviate fears and phobias in any area of life. I am so impressed with these therapies and exercises that I almost always integrate them into my coaching sessions.

NLP Neuro Linguistic Programming

I have often sat with other NLP practitioners to discuss how best to explain the concept of NLP. It is hard to explain, but I describe this process as using the senses, as opposed to thoughts, to facilitate and bring about change.

In saying this we can make subtle changes in things that we have experienced through our senses. For instance, we can take a bad memory of an unpleasant scene, and by changing things such as colors, clarity, size, or distance of where the image is in relationship to ourselves, or the orientation of the picture in our mind's eye, we can change the way we feel about the event.

We can use similar exercises around any of our senses. I guess you could say that NLP and similar exercises are therapy for the senses. There are many aspects to NLP, and it is a therapy which I personally love.

Thought Field Therapy (TFT) & Emotional Freedom Technique (EFT)

I first experienced TFT about fifteen years ago when I was suffering from debilitating panic attacks. I had tried so many things in an effort to overcome the anxiety and panic attacks but nothing had worked for me and I was desperate to find a solution. At this point I was open to try anything and as luck would have it I happened upon Dr. Lee Pulos, a psychologist who was at the time working with this relatively new therapy TFT.

In my first session I experienced this bizarre and almost playful therapy which instantly began playing a direct role in my overcoming the anxiety and panic attacks. I was so impressed with what I had experienced that I enrolled in a training program with Dr. Pulos, who was teaching the technique to a group of counsellors and mental health professionals. I was hooked by these fascinating techniques so took the opportunity to participate in advanced training which includes The TFT Boot Camp through Roger and Joanne Callahan.

During the training we learned how to diagnose treatment points by using muscle testing to get feedback from the body. Then using the feedback we were able to treat the appropriate therapy points. My sister (who was going through the training with me) and I questioned why we wouldn't simply treat all of the treatment points, and as it happened we were not the only ones thinking this way.

Gary Craig, who had also trained in the original practice of Thought Field Therapy, developed by Dr. Roger Callahan, developed a program which treated all of the treatment points. He called his program Emotional Freedom Technique or EFT. Now when working with a client I usually teach how to treat all of the treatment points as it is simpler to work with. We will do the same for the purpose of this book. You can learn more about TFT by visiting my coaching website www.suzanneprice.com

As impressed as I was with what I had learned in NLP, TFT and EFT, I found that, by combining these exercises along with other mind/body therapies I was able to completely overcome any anxiety, panic attacks, fears and phobias, as well as other negative or limiting beliefs which I had developed along the way. I've also now developed my own model called Tapping Into Your Mind Body Magic.

As horrible as it was to have suffered with anxiety and panic attacks, I know that I probably would never have encountered these therapies if I had not personally had this experience. It has been through the practice of these and other mind/body therapies that I have now been able to confront and overcome any obstacles which would have in the past prevented me from succeeding in any area of my life.

Many of you reading this book probably do not suffer from intense anxiety, panic attacks or phobias. However it can often be the low lying fears, negative beliefs and avoidance behaviours which hold us back. And, since these issues do not have a strong enough hold on us to become debilitating, we ignore them and let them control our lives anyway.

If you suffer from the fear of rejection or a fear of approaching someone you are attracted too, no matter how intense or mild it may be, if that fear is stopping you from going after who or what you want in your life then it is still controlling you. The bottom line is that fear and avoidance will always sabotage your happiness and the potential to find true love unless you learn to overcome it, and that is precisely what I'd like to help you with.

How TFT and EFT Work.

TFT and EFT treatments are largely based on, and incorporate exercises which balance life energy in the body. This type of practice is often referred to as acupressure, similar to acupuncture except the treatment points are stimulated by tapping or rubbing. And the exercises are usually taught to and performed by you, the client.

You may know of this life energy by the name of Chi. Chi is the universal life force that flows through the electrical circulatory system of the body. Chinese medicine considers a state of well being to be achieved by balancing these energy systems leaving the body in a state of harmony. The same could be said for our emotional balance.

Put very simply, Chi flows through 12 energy meridians. Each of these meridians has a corresponding major organ as well as a positive and a negative emotion. Chi energizes each of these organs. Balancing Chi is often referred to as Energy Medicine. What we are concerned with here is balancing the energy systems to release the stress which would be caused by the fear of rejection.

Releasing Your Past Into History

Although it may seem common sense that our past experiences have created who we are today, not all of those experiences were useful. Some of them even create negative anchors. This means that whenever we think about a bad memory, perhaps about a time when we felt rejected by someone we were attracted to, it may seem as if the feelings associated with that event has come flooding back into our mind/body system.

These anchors then become attached to similar events and get triggered whenever we want to approach someone who we are attracted too. Then, without realizing it the negative feelings that have become associated with such an experience, come flooding back, often preventing us from taking action.

If these memories still create misery or if the experience was so harmful that it created a negative or fearful anchor and caused damage to your self esteem, it is best to put that particular experience behind you once and for all. By doing so, you will eventually be able to release any negative feelings or anchors associated with the memory. This in turn will often allow you to see the situation in a whole different light.

A past rejection is definitely something that I would suggest you put behind you. There is no benefit to reliving the misery over and over again and allowing it to control your life in similar future situations. And, the thought that you might be rejected in a similar manner again will usually have little or no positive outcome for you. In fact, it can be a real motivation killer. So now would be a good time to stop those past experiences of rejection from controlling you, once and for all.

I call the following exercise - Releasing Your Past Into History. It is a very simple yet powerful tool and is the first step in the right direction to letting go of old hurts. You can use this exercise on any issue you want. It may be an old memory or a negative thought, feeling or experience that you have encountered in the past that still brings up bad feelings when you think about it now. Or, it may be an old reaction to a new experience that can spoil an experience that might otherwise be pleasant.

When an old memory affects you in such a negative manner, no matter what you think or feel about the experience it is very unlikely that you will be able to turn it around and produce a positive outcome from it unless you first detach the negative feelings that have become associated with it. And since these old memories only hurt you, your own personal health, and any prospect of forgiving or reconciling with someone, you need to put them behind you once and for all. The following exercise is very powerful and will help you do just that.

This exercise will not erase a memory, however it should help you to simply feel much less emotionally charged when you do think about it, or encounter a similar future experience.

Exercise - Releasing Your Past Into History

Think of a time when you had an encounter with someone that left you feeling uncomfortable. Just to give you an example, this may have been any experience which ended with a negative outcome leaving you feeling mistreated, angry, or hurt. To start with, try to pick an experience that was not too devastating.

When you think about this experience, notice how you felt when it happened. What were your feelings at the time of the event? As you think back about the actual event, on a scale of 1-10, with 1 meaning that you feel relaxed and 10 meaning that the emotions were very intense, where on the scale of 1-10 were your emotions at the time the event happened?

As you recall that event, and using the same scale of 1-10 what is the level of intensity of emotion associated with that memory now, in present time? It is very likely that you feel much less emotionally charged now. But if you still get upset when you think about it, I recommend that you do this exercise on this memory, as it is likely it still has somewhat of a hold on you now even if you are not aware of it.

Now, as you access that memory again, pay attention to the picture that you have of it in your mind. Imagine the scene as it played out in real life and take note of whether or not you can see yourself in the picture. Is it as though you are a witness or a camera on the wall watching it all unfold, and seeing yourself in the scene, or are you seeing the whole scenario unfold again, as if you were actually back there in that moment in time and seeing it all through your own eyes, just as you did when it happened?

If you can see yourself in the picture, you are dissociated. It is as if you are a bystander watching the event of which you were a part of. If you see the event as if you are seeing it through your own eyes, just as you did when the event took place, this means you are associated. In an associated state it is more likely that you will re-experience intense feelings when you think about that memory.

Now take that picture which you have in your mind and move it away from you, if you like you can even put it up on a movie screen in front of you. Practice changing the picture from being associated to being dissociated and switch back and forth.

Now, seeing the picture in its entirety, as if you could, hit the pause button to stop the motion and freeze the frame. Then, take that picture and shrink it down to the size of a piece of paper, scrunch it up in your hand and finally toss it up over your head into the air behind you. Throw it as hard as you can and let it go off into space. Visualize it taking off into the universe behind you, knowing that you are releasing that experience and it will continually distance itself from you.

Do this exercise on both pictures, the one that is associated (seeing it through your own eyes), and the one that is disassociated (seeing yourself in the picture as if you were watching a movie of the event and you were a performer)

If after doing this exercise you think about the event and the picture pops back up into your mind again, that's fine. Just scrunch it up and toss it back over your head again. Then change state by taking a deep breath, move around, drink some water and think about something that makes you feel happy. Just keep in mind what I mentioned before, this exercise does not remove the memory of what happened, but instead helps to detach or dilute the intense emotional feelings that were associated with it.

You can do this as many times as you need to and you can use it on any negative thoughts or experiences that you would like to change. This is such an easy exercise, but you will be amazed at just how less intense those negative emotions will be when you think about those past negative experiences again in the future.

Note: Please do not use the exercises in this book to attempt to diffuse trauma. Seek the assistance of a professional to support and guide you through the process.

Once you have done this exercise a few times, you will really be on your way to clearing some mental space with which you can develop some new and more powerful emotional resources. Now that we have done some work on putting those past negative experiences behind you, it is time to focus on how to change your behaviors, thoughts and feelings in future situations.

The following exercise is based on TFT or EFT. Both are very fascinating processes and if you wish to learn more about them, I will have some exercises, books and programs available on my coaching website www.suzanneprice.com

Relieving Symptoms of Fear or Stress Associated With A Specific Problem Using Meridian Stimulation Therapy

Very often, even if a person says and truly believes that they want to overcome a fear, there is a resistance to letting it go. It may be that the person simply will not take the action necessary to clearing the fear, or it may seem as though there is something that is simply out of that person's control which prevents them from achieving this particular goal. Sometimes it's as if there is an unconscious part of you which is sabotaging you. This exercise is one of my favourites and probably the easiest exercise to help you eliminate that unconscious saboteur.

This exercise will help eliminate any self-sabotaging behaviours that may be present even if you are not aware of them. There is a video on my website demonstrating how to do this exercise.

For this exercise, using your index finger and the one next to it, all you have to do is simply repeatedly tap the karate chop point on the outer side of the hand while stating the following affirmation - I unconditionally accept myself even though I have a fear of (you fill in the blank by stating your fear). For example: I unconditionally accept myself even though I have a fear of making eye contact. Or, I unconditionally accept myself even though I have a fear of talking to strangers. Repeat your affirmation three times.

You can practice this exercise three or four times a day. It only takes a few seconds so just do it whenever you get chance. The great thing about this exercise is that you can literally do it anywhere and at anytime. You could even do it while waiting for a bus, sitting in traffic in your car or sitting at your desk. You can apply this exercise to any negative thought you have about yourself.

Another tip for whenever you are doing any of these exercises is to make sure that you are hydrated by drinking a glass of water before doing them.

Fear Busting Exercise.

Think of a situation that might happen in the future, which has in the past caused you to feel some anticipation or fear. An example might be when you want to speak to an attractive stranger or someone who you have a crush on. Now make a mental note of what would normally happen under these circumstances.

What would you be thinking? How would you be feeling? What about the situation would cause you to hesitate? Make a list of all of your negative thoughts and feelings so that you can identify each of them as separate aspects. By doing so, you can deal with each negative aspect separately to help diffuse them one at a time.

Now, taking one of those individual negative thoughts or feelings, I suggest that you do the following exercise.

There is a video demonstrating this exercise on my coaching website www.suzanneprice.com

You might want to practice the exercise a few times first before attempting to do it while thinking of the negative thought or feeling. When you have finished, repeat the process with each aspect or negative thought or feeling.

While doing this exercise it is important to remember to think about and focus on the problem. Again, you might want to practice doing the exercise a few times first before attempting to do it while thinking of the problem

Part 1

- Using your index figure and the one next to it, tap all treatment points about 15 times each while thinking of the problem. Please see diagram of tapping points at the back of this book.

    1. Beginning of eyebrow
    2. Outer eyebrow
    3. Under eye
    4. Under nose
    5. Under bottom lip
    6. K 27 beneath the collar bone, about 1" either side of where you would knot a tie.
    7. Underarm on both sides of ribcage, in line with nipple, about 6 inches below armpit

Part 2

- While still thinking of the problem - tap the brain balancer on the back of the hand, about ½" to 1" up from the base of the fingers, between the ring finger and the little finger. Tap continuously while performing the following sequence.

    Eyes open

    Eyes closed

    Eyes down right

    Eyes down left

Big circle right

Big circle left

Hum a tune

Count to 10 – then count backwards

Hum a tune

Part 3

- Repeat part 1 of exercise while still thinking of the problem
  Tap all treatment points about 15 times each

    1. Beginning of eyebrow
    2. Outer eyebrow
    3. Under eye
    4. Under nose
    5. Under bottom lip
    6. K 27 beneath the collar bone, about 1" either side of where you would knot a tie.
    7. Underarm on both sides of ribcage, in line with nipple, about 6 inches below armpit

By following the exercises thus far, you have now started to remove the negative obstacles which were developed as a result of past negative experiences. This was achieved by first putting your past negative experiences behind you, and then releasing the negative emotional blocks by using the meridian stimulation exercise. This process will start to unlock your fear response associated with the fear of rejection.

In the following pages you will start developing some powerful new resources which will help you to build confidence. Please follow the exercises in the order as they have been laid out as I have designed this program in a way that each exercise builds upon the last one.

Part Two

Become A More Confident Version Of Yourself

Chapter 5

Reinventing Yourself ~ Creating A New & More Confident You!

Now that you are aware of how your old habits, beliefs, and past negative experiences have prevented you from going after who or what you have wanted in the past, and you have learned some great new tools to help you put those experiences behind you and eliminate your fears, it is time to start recreating a more confident and powerful you. In particular it is time to reinvent yourself so that you can become the person you have always wanted to be in relation to, and for the purpose of, meeting a potential life partner and developing a rewarding and fulfilling relationship.

Perhaps without even knowing it we have all mastered the art of reinventing ourselves as it is something we do continuously throughout our lives. However, we are not necessarily always conscious of the fact that we are doing it, therefore some of the changes we make may not necessarily be for the purpose of bettering ourselves. The key to success in reinventing yourself is to be very aware of who or what you want to become, and then to plan and act accordingly.

Knowing exactly what we want to achieve is the essence of our goal. Attaining that goal will come about through achieving clarity and setting a plan. Finding this clarity is a great exercise in self awareness and a wonderful foundation on which we can learn to practice the art of self coaching.

Let's get started. The first part of this exercise is to create a clear picture of whom, or what type of person, you want to become. Remember that although this exercise can be used in any area of your life, for the purpose of working through this book I strongly suggest that you stay focused on the issue of becoming a more confident and resourceful person when meeting someone and turning that encounter into a date.

Start by writing a statement to sum up who you want to become, making sure that it is a statement that works specifically for you. Make the statement so that it addresses a situation or experience that you have had or may have in the future, but focus on the desired outcome that you want to achieve. Your statement may sound something like one of the following:

- ♥ I want to feel comfortable when I am in the presence of an attractive stranger, and I want to feel confident enough to make eye contact, smile and start a conversation.

- ♥ I want to feel confident enough when I am in the company of someone who I know and like or feel attracted to, that I won't avoid them or act aloof, but instead I will enjoy spending time talking and getting to know them, and will possibly even flirt with them in fun.

- ♥ I want to be confident enough so that when I notice someone is paying special attention to me, I can reciprocate by smiling and showing that I am approachable.

- ♥ I want to be a confident and gregarious person who has the ability to attract my ideal partner into my life.

- ♥ I want to be confident and approachable when I meet an attractive person that I would like to talk to and hopefully build a relationship with.

- ♥ I want to be confident enough to flirt and have fun with whomever I like.

- ♥ I want to feel confident and motivated enough, so that next time I see an attractive stranger I will confidently approach him/her and start a conversation. If they reciprocate favourably I will then ask him/her if I can buy them a coffee or better yet ask them out on a date.

- ♥ I want to feel comfortable enough with myself that when I meet someone that I like enough that I might want to consider spending my life with, that I will be able to really show them, or tell them how I feel. I want to be able to let my guard down, put it all out there, and allow myself to be vulnerable.

Your statement will become part of your goal so really make it about the person you want to become. Write it down and don't worry about the fact that you may not believe it is possible at this point in time. It is possible to dream or imagine anything, so just go with that for now.

Now that you have written your statement, let's take a look at what it's going to take to become the person you truly want to be.

With your new goal in mind it is time to become more specific. You need to identify what will be so different about the new version that you want to create of yourself, from the person you already are. Essentially you need to pinpoint the qualities and characteristics that need to change in order to create this new you. You need to know what aspects of yourself, in relation to the topic of dating and relating are not serving you well, and what aspects you would like to develop in order to become the person you want to be.

It's time for a little soul searching. Just keep in mind that you are focusing on creating a new you in the context of how you feel about yourself and how you act and respond when in the company of an attractive person who you would like to get to know and hopefully develop a relationship with.

Now is your chance to imagine becoming the person you have always dreamed about being. To have the confidence and presence that will attract the life that you want to live and the people you want to have with you. Now is the time to let go of old beliefs and past behaviours that don't work anymore, and to create and develop new ones that will lead you into a happier and more successful life. At least in the areas of becoming more confident and meeting the love of your life.

Self Discovery

Go to a place you enjoy spending time, such as a coffee shop or patio, or somewhere that inspires you. Perhaps somewhere that is a great place to people watch. Take some paper and something to write with so that you can create a list that will ultimately become your model for clarity of who you will eventually become. You can actually go onto my website www.suzanneprice.com to download some worksheets for this exercise if you wish.

On the worksheet you will see that there are two columns. The first column is labelled Move Away From and the second is labelled Move Towards. The reason that they are labelled with these names has to do with our motivation strategies. In brief, the way this works it that whenever we want change in our lives we either focus on what we want or what we don't want.

If we are focusing on what we want, we are using the strategy to move towards. Our thought process may be "what do I want and how am I going to get it?" Depending on how badly we want that change will determine our level of motivation.

If we focus on what we don't want we are using the strategy to move away. Again depending on how badly we want to get away from whatever it is that we are hoping to move away from, will also determine our level of motivation. However, if we use the strategy to move away, we have to consider the fact that we are putting a lot of attention on the thing that we don't want. And knowing that we get or attract more of what we put our attention on, we may end up getting stuck, or worse yet attracting more of that thing we don't want. *Think Law Of Attraction!*

It is likely that most of us use both of these strategies at different times and for different situations, but being aware of which strategy you use and which is most effective for you is a very valuable tool.

So, with this is mind, it is time to start creating your lists. In the first column marked Move Away From, start writing down any negative thoughts, feelings, beliefs or behaviours that you have typically experienced when in the company of an attractive person. Note all of these experiences that simply do not serve you well and have sabotaged you in the past, and that you no longer want to experience.

These old patterns have probably sabotaged, and if you let them, will continue to sabotage you and your efforts whenever you meet someone or spend time in the company of anyone that you want to get to know and go out on a date with. Take as long as you like with your list, and keep in mind that you can add to it later if you find additional things crop up over time.

Next it is time to move over to your Move Towards column. Look at the first item you entered into the

Move Away From Column. Then think about what new resource, being a positive belief, behaviour, thought or feeling you would want instead. Write down this new resource in your Move Towards Column. See example below.

Move Away From	Move Towards
Negative Beliefs, , Behaviours, Thoughts and Feelings That Sabotage You	**Positive Beliefs, Behaviours, Thoughts and Feelings That Empower You**
Avoid making eye contact -	Make good eye contact
Act aloof around someone I like -	Be friendly & approachable
Act buddy, buddy like a friend -	Act more flirty and fun

I'm sure you get the picture! As you move through your list and have acknowledged the thing you no longer want, put a line through it, as you have now replaced it with something new that you want instead. (A great little tip: when you have finished this entire exercise, go through the list of resources you no longer want, then using the Putting Your Past Into History exercise, put them behind you once and for all.)

Then, when you have finished with this list, think about any other qualities that you feel you want or would like to have to help you become that person you really want to be. In order to help you generate your list it may help to think about times when you have seen other people respond to these similar situation in a way that you would like to respond in the future. And write down what you think it was that they did that made the difference. What are those qualities they have that you would like to develop and integrate into your personality?

At this point I'm sure you can see how by generating these lists you can become clear about what changes you want to make, and how by breaking down the issues into little chunks you will be able to make the changes one little bit at a time.

After completing your lists, go through and label each item as one of the following: a thought, a behaviour, a feeling or an emotion. By identifying these you will see that by focusing on, and changing your thoughts you will likely change your behaviour, and in the event of changing your behaviours it is very likely that there will be a very positive shift in how you feel.

One thing to keep in mind when doing this exercise is that this process is about you. It is about what you want, who you want to become and what you want to change. Make sure that as you think about new resources and behaviours that you want, they are coming from the heart and not from someone else.

Sometimes, when we say that we really want something, or that we really want to change in some way but we are just not able to achieve that desired outcome, it is because we have some sort of underlying conflicting belief. These are often hard to detect on our own and this is an area that I often cover in a coaching session or may cover in some of my workshops. See my website for demonstration of exercise to integrate conflicting thoughts, beliefs or feelings.

Anchoring

From this point we are going to pay special attention to the thoughts, beliefs, behaviours and emotional resources that you would like to have. We will call these, "empowering resources." In particular, I want you to go through your list and identify what emotional resources you would like more of in your life, especially in regards to the issue at hand, meeting someone special and dating.

These resources may be things such as courage, confidence, excitement or happiness, or they may be behaviours such as to be more outgoing. Choose resources you would like to have available to you whenever you would like to approach someone, or communicate with someone who you would like to develop a relationship with. Then pick one of the resources from your list, as you are now going to start the process of installing it, just like you would install a new program onto your computer. Just imagine how you would feel if you had this internal resource readily available to you anytime you wanted it.

Now we are going to start focusing on positive states of being as we begin building your confidence with an exercise called anchoring. The process of anchoring is something that I learned when training in NLP. An anchor is something that triggers an emotional state. We have anchors in every area of our lives; some are positive and some are negative.

For example, if public speaking has caused you to feel nervous, or worse yet, terrified, then public speaking is a very negative anchor. Any thoughts that elicit feelings of fear or that overwhelm you are negative anchors. If the thought of asking someone out or approaching an attractive stranger causes you to hesitate and go into a state of fear or panic, then that is also a negative anchor.

If on the other hand, seeing or thinking about a loved one causes you to feel happy and joyful, then the thought or sight of the loved one is a positive anchor. Or if the sight of a fire burning in a lovely fire place makes you feel warm and cozy, that is also a positive anchor.

In saying this we have to remember that not all anchors elicit the same feelings for everyone. It depends on what our own personal experiences have been with the different anchors. That same fire burning in a fireplace that elicited a cozy and romantic memory or feeling for one person may bring back a state of panic and terror for another, who had perhaps seen something they loved being destroyed by fire.

The good news is that we do have the power and the means to change or create new anchors, which will in turn change our emotional state. I explained earlier how a negative anchor can be developed. Anchors can be created automatically but we can create them deliberately too, and the same goes for positive as well as negative anchors. We can also pull them apart. The goal here is to create some powerful and positive new anchors that you can call upon whenever you need them, which in turn will put you into a positive state.

There are actually three components that you need to be aware of when creating your new anchor. First, you need to be aware of what situation you would like to have the powerful new resource anchored to. For instance, let's use the example of wanting to have more confidence when you meet an attractive stranger. Second, you need to know what new resource it is that you want to have anchored. In this case we are going to anchor confidence as a powerful new resource. And third we need to create the actual anchor.

The anchor could be anything and involve any of the senses. In creating an anchor we may decide to use a kinaesthetic anchor which entails performing a specific action such as snapping your fingers together, or it may be something you physically feel such as touching a piece of your jewellery.

Or you could use an auditory anchor, meaning that you would probably say something to yourself such as, "I am confident." You could also have a visual anchor which would be something that you see, this could even be something you see in your mind, like a sign or color which you predetermined to be associated with having confidence in this situation.

And, finally, you could also use your olfactory system, in which case it would be the sense of smell which would trigger the desired anchor. In this case you may be wearing a certain cologne or aromatherapy product that induces the state of confidence and will put you in your desired confident state.

Again, choosing the anchor has to be whatever works best for you, and you can certainly use more than one anchor to bring out the same positive state.

This may all sound a bit confusing but it is actually very simple. In summary the exercise will go as follows:

What is the situation that you want to change?

In this example we want to be able to act differently when meeting an attractive stranger.

What do you want to be different; what new resource do you want to have when you meet an attractive stranger; how do you want to handle this meeting differently?

I want to be confident in this situation.

What will you use as an anchor to elicit this feeling of confidence?

I will say the words "I am a confident person" (auditory anchor); I will see in my mind's eye that I am acting confident, cool, calm and collected (visual anchor); and

I will gently snap my fingers and stand up straight (kinaesthetic anchor).

Now that you have created a visual, auditory and kinaesthetic anchor it is time to install your new anchor.

Since we are using the feeling of confidence in this exercise, think of a time or situation in your life when you felt very confident about something. If you can't remember a time, think of a situation where you know that you would feel confident. And if this is also a problem for you, think of a time when you saw someone else acting with the confidence that you want to install into your life.

As you think about this confidence, really get into the feeling, using all your senses. What does it look like, or how would you imagine that confidence to look? What was the situation that made you feel so confident, (try to remember all the details.) Remember how you felt, feeling so confident, and remember what you might have heard. Was it something that you said to yourself, like, "this feels great", or was it something that someone else said to you, such as, "you look amazing" or "you did an amazing job."

You can also add any other senses to the experience such as if there was a smell or even a taste that was associated with that moment. Really get into the positive experience of that time when you felt this confident.

Now, while really getting into the feeling and becoming completely absorbed in the memory, install your kinaesthetic anchor. Start by snapping your fingers and straightening up your posture. Then install your auditory anchor, saying in your mind, "I love feeling this confident," and install the visual anchor where you see yourself as that confident person. As you can see, this only takes a couple of seconds to do.

It is a really good idea to repeat this exercise a few times. Then if you like you can repeat the same process while thinking about different times or situations when you felt this confident. Do the exact same process, attaching those positive thoughts and feelings to your kinaesthetic, visual and auditory anchors. The goal here is to develop an automatic response to your anchors, so that when you fire off your kinaesthetic anchors by snapping your fingers and straightening up your posture, your auditory anchor by saying "I love feeling this confident," and your visual anchor, by seeing a powerful, positive vision of yourself, you will develop an automatic response of feeling this confidence again.

Then, when you find yourself in the presence of an attractive stranger, you can fire off your anchors again and this will help put you in a positive empowered state.

You can also repeat this exercise using different new positive emotions and powerful resources that you would like to have available to you at any time. You can make this anchor even more powerful by stacking more and more powerful resources to it.

To stack an anchor, it simply means that you do exactly the same process, but while thinking about a different empowering resource. Perhaps you want to feel enthusiastic as well as confident so you simply attach the additional empowering resource, feeling enthusiastic, to the same kinaesthetic, audio and visual anchors that you have already created for yourself.

Next you need to practice firing off these anchors. Like anything, this takes practice, so start to create some positive new anchors today. Then, throughout the day or tomorrow you can practice firing off your anchors by snapping your fingers and straightening up your posture, and then adding your auditory and visual anchors to see how strong those feeling of confidence return. The more you practice, the stronger the positive feelings will become.

There is one more step. Now visualize yourself in a future situation where you will have an encounter with someone you are attracted too. Fire off your anchors, feeling all of the powerful new resources that you just anchored, and visualizing yourself in this situation looking and feeling this confident. Repeat, repeat, repeat! This is how you truly create powerful new anchors.

Then, the next time you find yourself in a nerve-racking situation, such as wanting to approach an attractive stranger, you can fire off your anchors and bring back the feelings of confidence, and any other new feelings that you anchored along with it.

I used this method when I wanted to get into shape and was having a problem with my motivation. The anchors I used were colors. I decided that I needed to feel strong and determined and to have the stamina to get me through my workouts. I asked myself, "What color would be associated with being strong?" Immediately, a beautiful royal blue color came into my mind. I then asked what color would best represent determination, and a lovely turquoise popped into my mind. And finally I asked what color would represent stamina, and a beautiful bright pink popped into my mind.

Then, when I found myself at the gym, feeling bored and tired and wanting to go home, I would call on these colors, seeing them in my mind's eye, and sure enough I would have a great work out every time. The result was that I got into the best shape of my life.

Whenever we call upon past experiences, whether they are good or bad, just by thinking about them we automatically change the state we were in. The same goes for anything that we choose to imagine. We can daydream or have a fantasy about anything we like, and if it is a good experience in our mind it can make us feel really good or even euphoric.

The same happens when we think about something bad: that memory or imagined experience can put us in a foul mood. All of these thoughts, whether remembered or imaged are actually mind/body experiences. I'm sure you can see that a lot of what we feel throughout our day is actually created by our thoughts.

We have the power to have nothing but good days, and we also have the power to change how we will feel in future events that used to make us feel bad. You can practice now to have only good experiences whenever you approach someone that you find attractive.

To do so, all you have to do is visualize, daydream, imagine, or fantasize about situations when you might encounter someone that you find attractive, and in your mind see yourself with your newfound confidence. As you are doing this exercise, fire off the anchors you created. The more you use your mind to practice and rehearse, the better you are going to get at becoming a confident person whenever you want to talk to someone that you are attracted to.

You will never be able to be certain that the person you want to approach will respond to you the way you hope, but you can learn not to let it bother you if things don't go as planned. Just remember that people will pick up on your confidence, and confidence in itself is very attractive.

For all you sports fans, think about your favourite sports personality and the rituals they perform before their game, or perhaps the rituals your favourite pop star performs before they go on stage. This is exactly the same kind of ritual, only they want to win at their race or to have a great performance, and you want to chat up or respond to an attractive stranger.

Creating A New Identity

The next step to creating the new more powerful and resourceful you, is to integrate your new image into your subconscious so that this change becomes believable in your mind. We are going to do this with a visualization exercise.

The reason I think it is so important to do this part of the process is that if we have developed a lot of negative behaviours and patterns we eventually believe that is who we are. I found that when I overcame my anxiety and panic attacks, I no longer suffered the physiological and emotional symptoms; however I still had very ingrained beliefs about not being able to do the things that I had avoided even though I had done them before having the anxiety. This meant that I still found it a real challenge to get out there and live life the way I wanted to no matter how badly I wanted it. I realized that there was a part of the process missing so I worked on creating a new belief about myself using a visualization process.

I have created the following exercise especially for the purpose of building confidence.

Creating A Powerful Version Of Yourself - Visualization Exercise

You are standing under a street lamp when you notice someone walking towards you. This person is confident, reassured, and looks as though they really "have it together." It is someone who you admire and who you have wished that you could be just like them. Looking hard you can see that this person has all of the qualities and characteristics that are on your wish list and that you would love to have for yourself.

In the darkness, you cannot see precisely who this person is but you sense a certain familiarity. Struggling to see who it is walking towards you, you sense a certain excitement, and feel at ease with their presence. That perfect stranger walking towards you is somehow giving you strength, hope and a sense of power. As they approach you feel confident and empowered.

Now close enough to see this person in the light, you notice that he/she is really happy, content and confident and has become the person you always wished that you could be. You feel that happiness and contentment too. In fact you can feel the confidence and all of the other feelings you wished that you could experience. Then, as this person reaches the street light which is now shining down onto both of you, you recognize who it is.

Now, as you take a step towards this perfect stranger you can feel the energy, strength and confidence they exude. With a feeling of happiness, joy and pride, you realize that the perfect stranger is in fact…. YOU!

As you are doing this exercise, use your own list of powerful and positive emotional resources that you would like to integrate into your mind/body system, and attach them to the person in your visualization.

Take pride in knowing that you are now taking the steps to become the person you have always wanted to be. Just by recognizing and admitting what you want you have now started the process of becoming that person which you desire to be.

You can gain confidence, you can gain strength, you can change the way you look, the way you feel, the way you dress and the way you respond to others; you can live any life you want to live. You can continue to reinvent yourself by adding any new and powerful resources that you would like to add to your life. You can constantly be reinventing yourself until you become the person you really want to be.

Chapter 6

Developing The Habits Of A Confident Person

Even for people who are typically very outgoing and confident, making eye contact, smiling and initiating a conversation with someone they are attracted too can be somewhat of a challenge. But it is one that can be very easily overcome.

The following chapter will show you a step by step plan of how to improve your flirting and social skills so that you will become much more confident in this area.

If you are a very shy person start by reading through this chapter, then visualize yourself practicing these skills before actually attempting them. If while doing the visualization you find past negative experiences crop up in your mind, do the putting your past into history exercises on these negative memories. Then visualize the whole scene again, only this time, change the ending so that it plays out the way you would like it to. Use the same exercise for any negative self talk that crops up as well.

Then when you have done this a few times, visualize different scenarios where you would like to approach and talk to someone, and see the whole process play out the way you want it to - with a happy ending. You do have the capability to make anything turn out the way you want it to in your mind. So practice using positive scenarios.

If while visualizing future encounters you find that you still anticipate negative outcomes, try practicing the fear-busting tapping exercises from chapter 4 while thinking about the worst possible scenarios you think could happen when you approach someone you are attracted to. Then, after completing that exercise, replay the whole scenario in your mind but visualizing the positive outcome.

Sometimes when we have a fear, we have to ask ourselves, "What is the benefit to having it?" There is always a pay off, and it may be that there is another aspect which you have been or are avoiding. By getting rid of a fear, there is often a feeling or threat that we will have to confront whatever other aspects we have been avoiding. You may want help uncovering this underlying fear too.

Ask yourself, are you ready to let go of these old negative feelings and beliefs to make room for more powerful resourceful and rewarding behaviours that will ultimately help you get whatever you want out of life. If you are ready, then let's go.

It is said that it takes twenty one days to create a new habit, or perhaps twenty one times would be more the case, so make sure that you practice daily. But regardless of time, it is consistency in practice that counts. The payoff is that if you follow these simple guidelines and practice these social skills on a daily basis, these skills will gradually become easier until they become second nature to you and are no longer an issue. As you practice them, notice all of the ways that things are becoming easier for you, and the positive outcomes that you experience.

These are some of the skills you will need to practice and develop in order to confidently, **Turn That Next First Glance Into A Date.**

Make Eye Contact

Let me tell you a *little secret* about eye contact.

Have you ever noticed how sometimes when you are completely engrossed in whatever it is that you are doing, that for no apparent reason you suddenly look up, turn around or look into a certain direction to find that you are looking directly into the eyes of a complete stranger who just happened to be staring right at you? Have you ever wondered what made you look?

This is a very similar scenario to the one in which *you* have noticed, or been drawn to someone and can't seem to take your eyes off them. Perhaps they are someone you find attractive or are fond of, but you do your absolute best not to get caught peeking. Then suddenly that person who you were looking at, looks up and locks eyes with you.

In both cases it almost seems as though something made us, or them, look, right at that very moment causing us to make direct eye contact with each other. Do you ever wonder if there could be some sort of *energy* that brings people together just like that?

The fact of the matter is that whenever we make eye contact with someone, there is a very good chance that the eye contact was not our first point of contact at all. Since this is so fascinating and so relevant I will share a little scenario with you to help you understand why we may have made eye contact with someone in the first place.

Whether you believe it or not, we all have life energy flowing through and around our bodies, all of the time. Ever heard about how we are all connected?

Although most of us cannot see it with the human eye, depending on how in tune you are with your energy, we can learn to feel it and become more aware of it. This energy can actually be captured in images by using a special kind of photography called Kirlian photography.

Studies using this form of photography have shown that when a person walks into a room full of people, energy from the bystanders reaches out to check out the energy of the person who is entering the room. So by the time that you have made eye contact with someone, there is a very good chance that your energy and the energy of the person your eyes are locked with have already met. Then, for whatever reason, it prompted you to connect on a conscious level.

I say "conscious level" because this whole process takes place on an unconscious level, meaning that we are typically unaware of it happening. This unconscious act prompts us to make eye contact so that we become consciously aware of each other's presence. Thankfully our unconscious self never seems as shy as our conscious self. As I'm sure you have probably figured out by now, that if we let our conscious analytical brains decide everything for us, we may never end up actually connecting with anyone at all.

I personally find these energy processes incredibly fascinating and to me it makes complete sense. You, on the other hand, do not have to believe a word you read. However, it might be interesting for you to take notice the next time that you make eye contact with someone, whether it was that person watching you, or you watching them that prompted the eye contact in the first place.

The same thing happens when you have already made eye contact with someone and both of you keep looking back. You don't necessarily deliberately decide when you are going to look back at each other, it just happens. The problem arises when we are shy or nervous. Instead of allowing ourselves to make eye contact and go with the flow, we deliberately avoid looking back because we don't want to get caught in the act, and this breaks down the process of interaction between two people.

Knowing about how our energy plays a role in making people consciously aware of each other in the first place means that we might as well just give up on the act of avoiding eye contact, the process has already began so we just as well make the most of it.

Here's a fun little exercise. Sit in a coffee shop or somewhere there are people just sitting around. Just relax, perhaps with a book or a newspaper. Then, when you are feeling settled, pick someone out of the crowd and look at them, don't stare, but just browse over the top of your newspaper or book in the direction they are sitting. Then just watch to see how long it takes for them to look back at you. It even works if you focus on someone who is engaged in a conversation. You can break eye contact as soon as they look if you want, unless of course you want to smile and chat them up.

This exercise works best when you are more in tune with your own energy. If you are interested in learning more about this then I'd recommend learning a bit about qigong. You will also be able to find some useful tips on becoming more in tune with your energy on my site, SJP Coaching & Consulting, the website address is www.suzanneprice.com

Making eye contact is paramount when it comes to making a connection. When our eyes meet, not only is it a signal that we have made contact, but eye contact is likely the trigger that sparks that initial interest and feeling of excitement when we see an attractive stranger. Triggering a primitive part of our brain, eye contact can initiate the feeling of familiarity and affection, or fear, making us want to either approach or retreat from the person with whom we lock eyes.

The key to eye contact triggering a state of attraction lays both in getting caught in the act, and having friendly eyes. If when making that initial eye contact with an attractive stranger you deliberately look away and avoid looking back because you feel too nervous or shy, you will probably send them the message that you are not interested. This will likely shut down any further communication and put the other person off.

When we make eye contact with someone we are attracted to it actually sets off a whole series of chemical responses in the brains and bodies of both yourself and the person with whom we have made the eye contact with. When staring into a potential partner's eyes, perhaps while on a date, "feel good" chemicals such as phenyl ethylamine (or PEA) is released into the body giving us that feeling of being in love.

The key to making positive eye contact is all about timing and duration. Too long of a stare can trigger feelings of being challenged and set off feelings of fear. Keeping your gazes brief, especially to start with, but gazing back within a few seconds starts a natural process of flirting. Extending your glances with a smile will keep the process natural and friendly, but staring for more than a few seconds right off the bat can be perceived the wrong way.

Since we are always unconsciously reading each other's body language, one of the things we are also aware of is the direction of the other person's eyes. Our attention tends to follow our eyes so if someone's eyes are on you, you can bet that the person is definitely interested, but if their eyes are wandering elsewhere you might not have their full attention.

It is also noted that the more attractive we find someone, the longer we will take to admire them and take in what we have seen. If you do find yourself looking at an attractive stranger and getting caught in the act, it is ok to look away, as long as you return the glance again within a few seconds. This second look will send the message that you liked what you saw and that you are in fact interested. Each time you look back and your eyes meet, try to hold the gaze a little longer and if you smile when making eye contact with someone, it is as good as an invitation to approach or make conversation. Remember if they are gazing back at you, then they are probably equally interested too.

If you are shy about making eye contact this following exercise will help you overcome the problem in no time at all. Tip: if you are really shy, you can do the EFT fear reduction exercises from Chapter 4 before you go out and practice this exercise, but whatever you do, please get out there and do it. If nothing else, you will be perceived as a friendly and approachable person.

Exercise

It is time for you to get out there and practice making eye contact. Put yourself in a position where you know there will be a lot of people around and practice the following techniques. Pick people who you would feel comfortable practicing on, people who you do not consider intimidating. It doesn't matter who they are; the point is to practice these social skills. Then as you become more confident with making eye contact and approaching people, you can gradually select more attractive people to practice on. This exercise will help prepare you to act upon your instincts whenever you encounter someone attractive that you'd like to approach or flirt with in the future.

Put yourself in the way of people and into situations where you have to make a connection. It could be as simple as walking through a busy doorway. When someone gives way to let you through, make eye contact and thank them. Or you might decide to stop people out on the street to ask a question. Simply say "excuse me, please could you tell me the time" or ask directions, but make sure that you make eye contact when you are speaking to them. Then smile as you thank them.

Another great idea is to go to a place where there is perhaps a narrow stairwell or walkway where people have to give way to each other. If you let people through, smile and make eye contact as they pass you, if people are giving way to you, make sure that you look them straight in the eye, smile and thank them. As long as you smile and you are polite, eye contact has an amazing effect on people.

Develop An Automatic Smile Response.

Perhaps the single most important element to making communication welcome and friendly is the smile. I think that perhaps the very thing that makes a person attractive is how that person makes us feel when we are around them, and that could even be for a brief moment. Not only are smiles contagious but they are also the signal that tells onlookers you are friendly and approachable.

When you smile, little receptors in your cheeks send a message through your nervous system to your brain, telling it that you are happy, and this good news prompts the brain to send you a little gift of feel good chemicals in celebration of your happiness. This in turn makes you feel more relaxed. By developing an automatic smile response you are contributing to your own health as well as the wellbeing of those around you.

Developing an automatic smile response is easy; it just takes practice. It is as simple as walking past a co-worker, making eye contact and flashing a smile, even a little closed lip smile will do. It only takes a second and you can practice doing this right now, by visualizing it to start with. If you find doing this too intimidating, practice on kids or pets. Stop to pet a dog while out for a walk; as you are making a fuss of it smile, then look up at the owner, pay a compliment about the dog, or ask its name and then smile again, even if it is while looking down at the dog. Then transfer your smile back to the owner, making eye contact before saying good bye.

You can now add your smile response to your eye contact exercise. Smiling will actually make the act of making eye contact much easier because your smile will comfort the person you are looking at. The response you get will probably be more positive, too. So just follow your eye contact exercises above but add a smile to the equation then pay attention to the great responses you will get.

If you are really nervous don't practice these exercises on people you find intimidating, but pick people you feel you would be most comfortable with and then work your way up. If you like, you can practice the fear busting exercises that you learned in the first part of this book before attempting any of these exercises. You will soon notice how easy this becomes and how you will start to feel better about yourself too.

Strike Up A Conversation

OK… so you are tuned into your surroundings; you've made eye contact and you've even plucked up the courage to flash a smile. Now what? Well you don't want to let them get away after getting this far, do you? Now is the time to strike up a conversation, or at least pass a friendly comment that will have that person remember you because of it. And… if you have gotten this far, making conversation should be easy.

Just like anything else, conversation with a stranger takes practice. So when you are feeling confident at making eye contact, and you have learned to develop an automatic smile response you can layer on the next part of the confidence building exercise by striking up a conversation.

The part where most people seem to get stumped is wondering what to say, but if you just say the first thing that pops into your head, like hello! That would be a good start. If you are comfortable using humour, that is usually well accepted, otherwise make a comment that is relevant to the situation you are in, preferably a positive one.

Striking up a conversation can be as simple as making a comment or asking a question about what the person is doing, or wearing, or whatever you feel most comfortable talking about. If you are a shy person just make sure that you start practicing these skills on non threatening participants.

Personally, I enjoy talking to anyone. And, I find that most people welcome a little chit-chat, it just seems that very few people want to initiate the conversation. If I go for a walk by the beach and see an elderly person sitting on a bench alone, I will often stop and ask if they mind if I join them. They are great people to talk to and usually love the company, and I have seen myself sit and talk to an elderly person for hours.

Another great place to meet people is at a grocery store. It is easy to strike up a conversation in a line up, or by helping someone who is struggling to open one of those produce bags that were purposely designed not to be opened. Or if someone is picking out fruit you can nonchalantly start picking out the same fruit and, when you find a good piece, offer it to them, pretending that you just changed your mind about buying it.

Speaking of stores, if you are really shy a good place to start would be retail stores. The clerks are there to answer your questions so spend a few hours going around some of the retail stores speaking to the staff.

You have every right to be there and can ask them about different products, sizes, colors, whatever it takes. Just get chatting and practicing your social skills.

People with accents are also great to talk to as an accent is the perfect conversation starter. Simply go up and ask someone the time, or ask for directions and when they answer you, zone in on the accent then ask where they are from. You can carry on the conversation by complimenting them on their accent and ask what it is like where they came from.

You see the possibilities for making conversation are endless. And if you keep practicing, you will soon overcome your shyness, feel good about yourself and who knows you may even make some new friends along the way. People are typically friendly, but they may be just as shy as you are and are probably waiting for an invitation to talk.

I strongly suggest that you keep your conversations positive and upbeat, and focus on the other person so that you are not obsessing on how you are doing. If you still feel a bit nervous about initiating conversation then this may be a perfect time to fire off your powerful resources anchors that you developed earlier in the book.

When you have gotten the conversation going you will often come to realize that the other person is carrying half of the weight and you are not fully responsible to carry the conversation at all, so you can just go with the flow.

Very often, when we find ourselves with an opportunity to talk to someone we find attractive, the chances are that we only have a few minutes in which to act. By being aware of their body language you will be able to gauge how well things are going between you. If the person you are talking to is looking away, looking uncomfortable or giving negative verbal cues, you will more than likely get declined if you ask for their phone number or ask them out at this point.

If, when you start approaching people and talking to them you feel that the conversation is very one sided and you are doing most of the work, it is very likely that the person you are talking to is quite shy. In this case you are going to come across as the more confident one. If this happens, just keep the conversation very general. If you find that after a few attempts to make conversation that you are not getting a favourable response, you might be best to just let things go and find someone else to talk to.

Simply stay positive, calm and maintain your self respect. If on the other hand you are feeling confident that your conversation is going well and you want to ask the person out, then go right ahead. Just remember, the more you practice, the more confident you become, and when the right one comes along you will be ready to go.

Rehearsing these ideas in your mind is a great way to build confidence. Also take some time to think about the times when you did approach an attractive stranger, or anyone for that matter, and started a conversation which went well. If you can't think of any, what about times when you saw someone else do it? Perhaps it was even something you saw in a movie or on a show. Visualize yourself doing whatever they did, and learn to model, (observe and practice) the behaviours of those people that you would like develop for yourself. Always make sure that whatever you visualize yourself doing turns out to be a positive interaction with a positive outcome.

Chapter 7

The Secrets To Becoming A Super Attractive Person

Two major themes that often permeate throughout so many people's lives are the thoughts and feelings of either not being good enough, or of not being attractive enough.

Perhaps like deep dark secrets, these insecurities lie even beneath the fear of rejection. If not addressed, these negative thoughts and beliefs have the potential to prevent a person from ever experiencing true happiness, and could lead to a lifetime of loneliness by ultimately preventing that person from ever finding the love of their life.

If you are someone who suffers with these nagging negative thoughts, even if it is only once in a while, perhaps it would be a good idea to challenge your beliefs by answering the following questions:

- ♥ **What does being attractive mean?**

- ♥ **How do you know, where did you get this idea of what attractive is supposed to be?**

- ♥ **Who are you not attractive enough for?**

- ♥ **What makes you think that you are not attractive?**

- ♥ **What do you think you need to do in order to feel or become more attractive?**

There is a worksheet on my website to help you work through and challenge these questions.

It would be a good idea to answer these questions before you move on as your answers may reveal some beliefs you have that you weren't even aware of having. You may even discover that they have become significant obstacles in your life. Let's take a look at these questions.

- ♥ **What does being attractive mean, and whose interpretation is it anyway?**

If you feel that you don't measure up to what *you* think "attractive" is, you might take a little comfort in knowing that most people, at least some of the time, think and feel that they are simply not attractive enough either.

This problem may arise particularly if a person's interpretation of being attractive is based on an image of whom or what they think attractive should *look* like. And this would be a very natural way of thinking.

The danger about having a very specific idea of what attractive looks like is that if you don't resemble this image, there is a very good chance that you are going to feel insecure about the way you look. Sound familiar? If so, you need to be asking yourself, whose interpretation of being attractive is this anyway?

No matter whether it is your own personal idea or one that you have adopted from what you have seen on television or in a magazine, the fact of the matter is, not everyone is going to agree with you. That's right, because even though we hear about the stereotypical shopping list of what attractive is supposed to be, in reality most of us don't really agree with this at all.

Believe it or not, not every man wants a woman who looks like a Barbie doll, and not every woman wants a Fabio look-alike. Everyone has their own interpretation of what they find attractive, and very often it has little or nothing to do with *looks* at all.

However, even when it does come to that initial physical attraction, you might be very surprised at just what some people really consider to be *attractive*. For instance there are plenty of guys who spend hours working out at the gym to maintain a very fit and toned physique who don't necessarily look for the same in a woman. Most men still love curves and appreciate a feminine curvy body, a great smile and a positive attitude towards life.

Same with age, gone are the days where men want a younger woman. In fact there is a huge trend where younger guys are attracted to and want to meet and have a relationship with a woman who is more mature and comfortable with herself.

Also, it's not that uncommon to see an attractive woman with a very average looking man, and vice versa, or a taller woman with a man several inches shorter than herself. Perhaps there is more to this whole attraction thing than what meets the eye!

The fact of the matter is that at the end of the day, when you have met someone special, even though it was very likely physical attraction (whatever that might have been) that played a role in you getting together, it is not likely going to be enough on which to build a life-long relationship. It is the person as a whole, encompassing their personality, beliefs, lifestyle, passions and convictions, just to name a few that will cause someone to fall and stay in love. And that is *"real love"* that I am talking about. What a relief, right?

♥ Who Are You Not Attractive Enough For?

Not only do we like to measure ourselves up against unrealistic models of what we think "attractive" should be, but some of us also like to think that we know what the opposite sex finds attractive too. Or worse yet, what we think someone who perhaps we are particularly fond of may find attractive.

When we like someone we tend to put them up on a pedestal and often see them as something far greater than perhaps what most others would. And because we have this perhaps distorted or glorified image of who we think this person is our expectations of who we might expect them to like may be equally distorted too.

Then, if we don't have the greatest self esteem we may feel that they are out of our reach, and that we could never be good enough or attractive enough for them. Then, just to torture ourselves even more we also measure ourselves up against this completely unrealistic and imagined model of what we think *they* would find attractive.

This sort of insecure thinking will probably cause us to act in a way that we may come across as aloof or disinterested and in doing so we will probably send out the wrong message anyway. Thoughts and behaviors like this have a tendency of creating a self-fulfilling prophecy where we eliminate ourselves from the running of being with this person. This is a classic case of self-rejection.

Hmmm… I wonder if we stop to think about it, do we do this to ourselves because we think this person is so great, or is it because we think we are not good enough or attractive enough for them? By putting these obstacles in our own way we can keep a bigger distance and give ourselves a good excuse not to pursue them anyway.

If you have spent years thinking that attraction is only about looks you will really need to retrain your way of thinking. To do so you need to keep in mind that looks are only a small part of what makes someone attractive, even from a visual perspective.

As you read through the following chapters you will soon learn what it takes to become a "super attractive" person.

How To Become A Super Attractive Person.

Have you ever noticed how someone who you might not have typically thought of as being attractive suddenly turned out to be someone you can't seem to get out of your mind? Or what about a person who you had a brief encounter with, and for some strange reason you just can't wait to see them again? When we think about these people they lift our spirits and bring a smile to our face. And although we might not quite understand why, in one way or another we simply find them to be very attractive people. But have you ever stopped and wondered why?

Perhaps without realizing it, when you really think about what makes a person truly attractive, it is not how they look, what they wear, or what they do for a living, but it is in fact how they make us feel when we are around them. In other words, attraction has more to do with social skills, body language, behaviour and connection than anything else. And the good thing *is* that these skills can very easily be learnt. If we can learn to observe and then model some of the behaviours of popular and attractive people, we will also move ourselves into that category of being an extremely attractive person, too.

How To Develop A Magnetic Personality And Attract Others Into Your Life

To be an attractive person means that people are automatically drawn and attracted to you and they enjoy being around you because they like the way they feel when they are in your company. Becoming an attractive person is actually quite a simple process that starts from the very moment you first meet someone.

The truth is that we are all a little bit shy, at least in some situations, so if you push yourself to step out of your comfort zone and go out of your way to put others at ease then people will automatically be drawn to you. By being the first to break the ice and initiate others into a conversation or a group, and make them feel welcome and included, you will become someone that they will feel comfortable to be around. This alone will turn you into one of those people who can easily attract people into your life.

Many people are even a bit reluctant to acknowledge, or initiate a conversation with someone who they have already met in the past. Perhaps they do this because they don't really know each other well enough so they avoid one another out of fear of not being recognized. If you find yourself in this type of situation, take charge by at least acknowledging the other person with a smile, a wave, or if in close enough proximity, a simple hello.

By doing so, you are letting the other person know that you do in fact remember and recognize them. This simple act will make that person feel respected and important enough to you that you remembered them. People like to be recognized and your acknowledgment will be considered favourably as we consider thoughtful people to be easy to be around and, therefore, also attractive.

Talk to the people you have seen around on a regular basis. We all know of people who are very familiar to us but we have never actually formally met. We may see them at work, on the bus or in a local coffee shop and we see them on a regular basis, but nobody has taken that step to say hello.

I actually find this behaviour quite bizarre as it seems insane that we frequent the same places, see the same faces, and yet nobody actually talks to each other. Sometimes you have to just bite the bullet, throw caution to the wind and start a conversation. Even when you do so, it is very likely that the next time that person sees you again they may still avoid you because they have now turned into a "familiar avoider". But, just make the effort, say hello, ask how they are doing and see where it goes. It doesn't hurt and it only takes a minute, so why not make developing a social planet part of your daily routine.

These familiar faces are potential friends and yet we ignore each other probably because we either don't want to intrude or we are afraid of not being recognized. However, considering the fact that humans are typically very social beings, I would bet that most people would probably love the fact that you took the time to interact with them and would be happy to have a chat.

If on the other hand we all just sit back and wait for everyone else to make the first move and take the initiative to acknowledge us and start a conversation, we are then also contributing to that semi anti-social behaviour. If you make the effort to be the first one to say hello and in turn make everyone else feel special, guess who becomes the attractive one?

When meeting new people, be genuinely happy to make their acquaintance, and then be equally enthusiastic to acknowledge them whenever you interact with them again in the future. Be the first to greet them and ask how they are, and be genuinely interested in their answer. Make the conversation about them, not only will this make them feel more important but it will give you the opportunity to feel more relaxed as you have taken the attention off yourself.

Always be respectful of others no matter who they are, and learn to be perceptive. We are all natural experts at reading other people's body language so be aware of who you are interacting with and build rapport by matching similar body language where appropriate. If you notice someone is nervous or shy, go out of your way to put them at ease and make them feel relaxed and comfortable in whatever environment you are in.

When having a conversation with someone put your focus on them and give them your undivided attention. And don't be afraid to ask questions about what they are telling you. Acknowledge what others have to say and participate in their conversation. Be conscious not to step in and change the conversation to another topic as soon as they stop for air. If you want to change the conversation try to give some feedback on what they are talking about before gently bridging the conversation into a new topic.

One of the best ways to be attentive is by maintaining good eye contact. If you find your eyes wandering you will easily become distracted and rapport will be broken making the other person feel uncomfortable and unwelcome.

Pay genuine compliments and praise where appropriate, and accept a compliment with a simple thank you. It's great if you can add a little story about whatever you are being complimented on as long as it doesn't cross the line to boasting or bragging.

Use good manners and refrain from becoming too familiar with someone until you have had the opportunity to assess each other, and have started to build a good rapport. Make sure you are both comfortable with each other and refrain from laying out your entire life story of doom and gloom with people you have just met. Keep your conversation light and positive, and save your sob stories for your best friends, therapist or your hairdresser.

Be respectful to everyone. It doesn't matter who you are dealing with, everyone deserves respect. And even if you don't think so, you are likely being judged by how you interact with others. There is no better way to see the true character of a person than how they treat those around them. If you are with someone who is mistreating another or using what they perceive as their authority or right to treat others with disrespect, don't make the same mistake by following suit. This is definitely one of those situations where you don't want to match another person's actions.

When making an exit, do so politely. Excuse yourself, thank people who have served you and acknowledge everyone with whom you interact with. Whether it is the doorman, a waiter, a shop clerk or the person with whom you are doing business, treat everyone fairly and with respect. Leaving a positive impression wherever you go will turn you into an incredibly attractive person.

As you can probably see from the examples above, becoming an attractive person has as much if not more to do with acknowledging, interacting and connecting with others than it does with looks. How you act in these areas will have a huge impact on how others *see* you. These behaviours all contribute to what we consider to be "physical attraction", only we are often not aware of how much of an impact our behaviour and social skills have on how others, including onlookers, see us. By practicing these skills you truly can increase your odds of becoming a super attractive person.

Chapter 8

You May Never Get A Second Chance At Love At First Sight

Ah! Love at first sight. What a lovely thought, and one that often has many people wondering about that age old question. Does love at first sight really exist? I for one would like to believe that it does, and if I am right, then we had better be ready for it to happen anytime and anywhere.

I would be the first person to admit that it is very possible to become attracted to, and fall in love with someone you might not have originally thought of as being attractive. After all, it is often how a person makes us feel that will ultimately capture our hearts. However, since we are talking about "love at first sight" the very thing that is going to cause sparks to fly will be that initial physical attraction.

This attraction happens when something about you fits into your admirer's model of what he or she considers beautiful, attractive, or good looking. And the same happens in reverse too. Since everyone has their own interpretation of what attractive is, you definitely do not have to be a supermodel for this to happen to you.

We all have certain things that capture our attention and that we find attractive. It could be anything from the shape of someone's body, or the look on their face, or even the coloring of their skin and hair. Or it could be something completely unrelated to their actual physical appearance, and may have more to do with a person's body language, mannerisms or the way in which they move.

Love at first sight could even be initiated by something like how a person treats or interacts with those around them. And although these are not necessarily physical characteristics per se, they are still all part of a person's visual profile.

So as you can see, visual or physical attraction, as it is more commonly referred to may have a lot more to it than just having a pretty face. And although there is definitely no such thing as one size fits all when it comes to attraction, there are a few things that most people would agree on that they would find appealing about someone of the opposite sex.

Superficial or not, there are certain traits about the opposite sex that most of us would agree that we find attractive. And yet many of these traits may be nothing more than minor details which represent how that person feels about and portrays themselves. However they may ultimately represent what the onlooker considers sexy, mysterious, powerful, or whatever the case may be. The fact that we judge people by such traits is more often than not, just basic human nature.

So, with this in mind, maybe we should look at what we can do to possibly increase our odds at finding that love at first sight.

Consider this. Within approximately seven seconds of seeing a complete stranger we usually form an opinion about them on many levels. We do this and yet we probably have not even talked to each other at this point. And as we are giving them the quick "once over", guess what they are doing to us. This ritual may mean not only that you get just one chance to make a great first impression, but also more importantly, when it comes to meeting your Mr. or Miss. Right, you may only get just one chance at love at first sight.

When it comes to physical attraction, even though it may be a person's hair, clothes, body shape, body language and facial expressions that will first grab us, it may often be the little details that will sway our opinions.

Depending on what criteria you use to measure a stranger by, an individual's appearance may account for approximately fifty to ninety percent of what a first impression is based on. The remaining ten to fifty percent (depending on how much weight we personally put on the first visual appearance) is based on voice tone and tempo, and the remaining few percent is based on what we have to say. The problem with this is that no matter how smart or quick witted you may be, you may never get the chance to prove yourself if you don't pass the visual test first.

Have you ever had one of those regretful experiences where you encountered an attractive stranger but you kind of wished you hadn't? You know, like the time you just crawled out of bed on a Saturday morning and threw on a pair of your tatty old sweats to run down to your local coffee shop to pick up a vanilla latte.

Looking like you had been dragged through a hedge backwards you buried your head in a magazine hoping you wouldn't bump into any one you knew. But as you waited in line with one eye on the door to check out who was entering the scene you turned around and were pleasantly surprised to find your dream lover standing right behind you.

Well... Ding Dong! Could this be your lucky day? Obviously you both drink coffee and both of you appear to be alone, and since you are already in the coffee shop and in close enough proximity to start a conversation, what a perfect opportunity for a quick chat up, or flirting session!

Suddenly aware of your less than flattering appearance, you realize that if you dare attempt to say hello now, you would probably just scare your Mr. or Miss Right off anyway. So, regretfully, you make the decision to remain anonymous at least for the time being. Then, as you slither past hoping he or she won't notice you, you wonder if you were to show up again the same time the following day if you might be in for a better chance for a more positive encounter.

This is a very realistic and disappointing scenario, and although probably a bit of an exaggerated circumstance for most of us, many single people leave the house without making any effort at all to prepare themselves for a surprise encounter.

What if you bumped into that special someone while out walking your dog, shopping at your local grocery store, or even sitting on the bus? It wouldn't be unheard of to meet the love of your life while riding in an elevator, or even pulled up alongside each other at a traffic light. So if you found yourself in one of these situations, would you be ready to act?

Knowing that you could literally bump into your Mr. or Miss Right anywhere and at anytime, it might be a good idea to think about the efforts you make whenever you go for an evening out in the hopes to meet that someone special. Then, if you start to apply some of the same grooming and preening rituals to your daily routine, you might start to attract a little bit more of the right kind of attention to yourself.

Consider this: if you were going to go out for an evening, perhaps to a bar, a dinner party or a singles dance, hoping to meet some potentially eligible love candidates, what extra measures would you take to make sure you were going to get noticed and stand out in the crowd? And what is it that you would do to make sure that you make a great first impression?

If you were serious about meeting someone, the chances are that you would take the time to make sure you looked great, were well groomed, and dressed in a fashion that would allow you to stand out in the crowd. Wouldn't you do whatever it takes to make sure that you would stand a good chance against your competition?

So ask yourself this: if you are willing to spend the time to go to all of this effort for a night out on the town, why are you not taking the same steps in your daily routine? By doing so you could ensure that you would stand the same chance of getting noticed, and you would probably start attracting the kind of attention that you want from the people you want to attract, anywhere and anytime.

If you really want to meet that someone special you have to be prepared for it to happen anywhere and at any time, and it doesn't necessarily mean that you have to spend a lot of time in the mirror. It does however mean that you do need to take care of a few basic details.

Like it or not the first thing that a person is consciously aware of is our appearance. If they like what they see they will not only look longer but they will also be far more likely to take a second look. Our appearance encompasses the whole package, which includes how well we are put together, how we hold and carry ourselves, our body language and basically how we behave and interact with others.

Perhaps from now on we should think of ourselves as our own best or worst self-marketing tool because you are literally a walking billboard. So if you want to make every encounter count, you can start by making the effort to put yourself out there for the whole world to see, and if you do it right, those who are looking will stop to take notice of you.

This of course doesn't mean that you have to get all dressed up like the dog's dinner to go for a walk or to hang out at a coffee shop with friends. I always say, dress appropriately for any occasion, pay attention to the details, and act in a way that will make people like you. This is how you get noticed and attract the kind of attention you want. It is very easy to make a positive statement about yourself and in doing so you will benefit from the affirmative effects of an added boost of confidence, a feeling of self-respect and shot of sex appeal.

Get Into The Habit Of Looking Good.

If you are single and looking to meet your Mr. or Miss Right, you might want to get into the habit of checking yourself in the mirror every time you are about to step outside of your door. Make sure that you look your best at all times.

Keep a mirror close to your front door and take a look to see what others see, smile, straighten up your posture, make sure everything is in order and that you look and feel confident. Look once, do a little spin to the right and look again, finally a spin to the left and look again…if all looks good, get out there and present yourself to the world. You need to be seen so make sure you are looking your best for whenever that happens.

From a visual point of view, besides the obvious of taking a shower and smelling and feeling fresh, you only need to take care of a few minor details that will help you to stand out in the crowd. If you look good, others will see a person who respects and takes care of them self. They will think you have got it together and in turn they will have more respect for you. If you look dishevelled you will likely feel washed up and may literally become invisible to anyone looking for love.

Guys are often particularly attracted to feminine women and it can be the minor details that count. Men notice details such as nice hair, nails and the color of the lips. So ladies, use a bit of mascara and lip gloss and get a manicure. In the eyes of a man these little details will go a long, long way. To him you will literally exude femininity and sex appeal.

Women on the other hand tend to notice how well a man is put together. It doesn't mean that you have to leave the house in your best Armani collection to get noticed, but do make sure those great jeans and t-shirt or sweater fit well, are clean, pressed and in good condition. If you really want to stand out in the crowd, wear dress shoes, not sneakers or gym shoes. In fact dress shoes should be an absolute must. And, by the way, we can tell the difference between the bed head look and actual bed head. It doesn't take a lot of time so make the effort and you will soon see that it is worth your trouble.

My point being that you have to be ready to bump into your Mr. or Miss Right at anytime, anywhere, and in any situation. And especially remember that you may never get a second chance at love at first sight.

What Does Your Appearance Say About You?

I have met and worked with a lot of people who have adopted the attitude that it is shallow to be concerned about how you look. And then they usually say something like, "Well, they can take me or leave me, if they don't like the way I look then they can look elsewhere." Hmmm… well, that's fair enough if you want to think that way. The only problem is, it may be partially due to this attitude that will cause you to be left on the shelf. It is also conceivable that if you don't make the effort, any would-be potential suitors might go looking elsewhere.

So, if you are serious about finding the love of your life then perhaps you will need to change your attitude about your appearance and the image you portray. Remember, your image speaks volumes about how you feel about yourself and what type of person you are.

How Do You See Yourself, And How Does This Make You Feel?

First impressions are very important because how you represent yourself will not only determine how others see you but will also play a huge role in how you feel about yourself. If you like what you see you will probably *feel* confident and proud, and this will have a positive impact on how you act. If people pick up on the fact that you are confident, they will ultimately show you more respect.

Here are some basic tips to help you look and feel your best so that you too can make a great first impression.

Hair

In the hair industry we say that fashion is what you wear on your head, and on your feet, everything else is merely an accessory. Our hair is our crowning glory. Hair frames the face accentuating it shape and structure, and when cut properly it can enhance your best facial features. The style that you choose can say volumes about your personality.

Hair is something that we love to look at, touch and play with, and it doesn't matter whether it is our own or someone else's. Keeping it clean and maintaining the style is of utmost importance. Healthy, shiny hair represents youth and vitality so if you want your hair to speak positively about you, it is paramount that you keep it looking clean and healthy.

Hair color is also very important, and if you are coloring your hair be sure that you talk to a professional stylist or colorist to see what color best suits you and your skin tone. A good color should add shine and luster to your locks while enhancing your overall look. However, if color is a new idea to you, be sure to consider your personality as well as your overall look before making any radical changes. Your best bet would be to only trust your hair to a well trained and reputable stylist.

Thinning hair can cause concern for many men and women but there are options available to help you with this. If you have not been blessed with lustrous locks, all is not lost. With hair extensions and very natural hair pieces made from real hair, there has never been a better time for alternative hair options for both men and women.

If you are a guy who is not interested in considering these alternative hair options and you like to shave your head, I have good news for you. It seems that most women are not at all put off by this trendy style of grooming, which has become so popular now that we often don't even notice if there's nothing there at all.

Skin

Clear, fresh and glowing skin is another indication of your youthfulness and good health. As they say, your skin is a reflection of what is going on inside. A measurement of vitality, you can achieve glowing skin largely by living a healthy lifestyle. Skin needs plenty of hydration so drinking plenty of water and avoiding too much caffeine, sugary drinks and alcohol is a good start.

When it comes to diet, make sure that you eat plenty of fresh fruits and vegetables and avoid indulging in a lot of processed foods. Your mental and emotional health also plays a huge role in how your skin will glow so getting enough sleep, exercise and fresh air will also help you look your absolute best.

Good skin care doesn't have to be complicated or expensive, but you should pay attention to more than just the skin on your face. Body lotion can keep your skin smooth and supple but make sure you use good quality moisturizer for your face, hands and neck.

When it comes to skin care I am a huge advocate for natural products. Just keep in mind that when something claims to be natural or organic, you have to consider what has been left *out* of the product, not what they put *into* it. Adding some herbs into an already toxic concoction does not make a product natural.

If you haven't already done so, take a visit to a good natural health store or aromatherapy shop and check out all of the options they have available. You can buy everything from body butters and massage oils to shampoos and conditioners, and even natural cleaning products for your home. Make sure to ask which products are synthetic and which are natural, then whenever possible go with the natural one, it will be much healthier for you.

When it comes to shampoos, ask about the base of the shampoo. The petroleum based products used in many commercial shampoos might be linked to some very serious diseases such as cancers. The downside to some natural shampoos is that they have less lathering action, but this is a good thing.

Great Teeth & A Nice Smile

One of the most powerful gestures that a person can make to positively affect those around them is to smile. A smile is like an invitation that warrants an immediate response and lets others know that you are friendly and approachable. And there is nothing like a great set of teeth to give you the confidence to smile.

Unfortunately we are not all blessed with nice straight teeth, but as long as you practice good hygiene, have fresh breath, and keep your teeth as white as possible you should be set.

Keeping the mouth clean by brushing after every meal and before bed, flossing and using mouth wash should be included in your daily routine. A salt water rinse or a natural mouth wash (ask an aroma therapist for suggestions) can help to kill any oral bacteria.

Teeth whitening systems can be purchased and used at home to keep your teeth nice and white on a daily basis or you can now get them whitened at a very reasonable price at practically any dental office.

Eyebrows

Eyebrows are definitely an important face-defining feature and need their own grooming and maintenance regime. Maintenance may include tweezing, cutting and coloring. If you are not sure how to do your eyebrows it is definitely worth getting them professionally groomed by an aesthetician, or if they are really long and bushy you can have your stylist trim them when you go for your haircut. If coloring your eyebrows, I definitely recommend you get them done professionally as you do not want to get hair color in your eyes. Never attempt to color your eyelashes yourself as the product used in these services can cause blindness.

Welcoming Hands

It is really funny but I, for one, after noticing an attractive person based on initial appearance, tend to be very drawn to the hands. I think for me it is more about the body language aspect, as how you respond and gesture with your hands can offer real tell tale signs of your personality, stress level and grooming habits.

Well-kept hands with nicely manicured nails tend to show the world that you have the ability to practice self-control and take good pride in your appearance.

Bitten nails with skin that has been picked at around the nails along with clenched fists may indicate a very uptight and perhaps angry person.

On a woman, soft hands and well manicured nails portray femininity, and depending on the style of manicure the nails can be considered to be very sexy. These are some of the little details that men pay attention to.

On a man (depending on his career), freshly manicured nails show self-pride and good grooming habits.

Hand cream, again, go natural. You can buy all your body basics and treats from a good aromatherapy or health food store. Think of it this way you are treating your body with something natural, you are protecting the environment, and you are speaking out against animal testing.

Hair Removal

There's a time and a place for everything, (well almost everything), and unwanted facial and body hair in most cases would definitely be an exception to the rule as there is no time or place for it. But the good news is that there are many ways to get rid of it, although some methods offer only temporary relief.

You can do a lot of your hair removal maintenance at home, and this is often much more convenient and of course more affordable. With shaving, waxing and chemical hair removers available, you have to pick the best method for you. No matter what claims are made by these product companies, all of these methods leave the hair capable of growing back so I would recommend the safest procedures for home use.

Other than the potential to cut yourself, shaving is probably the most convenient method of home hair removal. You can use an electric shaver or you can use a basic wet shave with a razor, most of which are pretty safe as long as you keep your wits about you. I like the idea of shaving because you can keep up with this method on a daily routine without any additional mess.

For best results when using a wet shave method, make sure that your skin is wet first and then apply a good shaving crème or gel (follow product directions on the can). Then in a uniform pattern carefully shave the desired area.

Waxing can leave a nice soft finish but whether you are waxing at home or getting it professionally done you have to use caution to make sure hot wax is not too hot, and you have to make sure the area is very clean. A lot of people suffer with severely irritated or infected skin from waxing mistakes.

Chemical hair removers are popular, but something I personally do not like. I don't like to think of anything that has such strong chemicals in it that it can disintegrate hair to be anywhere near my body. Nor do I want it going down the sink and polluting the environment.

Professional hair removal services include electrolysis and laser hair removal. I like the results of electrolysis but it is seldom permanent or at least not until you have had quite a lot of treatments. It can also be quite expensive in the long run and as the saying goes, no pain-no gain

Laser hair removal is probably one of the most popular treatments now and although I have not tried it myself I have seen some excellent results. Laser hair treatments seem to work best on strong, dark hair but the results may not be as promising with lighter, fairer hair.

Smell Fresh Not Fake

Gone are the days when people doused themselves in strong perfumes to cover up odors brought on through infrequent bathing, but unfortunately there are some people who still have not got the message. When it comes to scents you have to remember that not everyone experiences smell in the exact same way as you do. So what may smell good to you may be overpowering or downright offensive to someone else. Perhaps the most unfortunate thing about this is that most people would not want to offend you by telling you that your perfume is too strong, instead they may just avoid you altogether.

There are so many people who are now allergic to perfumes and colognes that many schools, universities, hospitals, gyms, work and public places, including some public transportation systems, are promoting or demanding perfume-free environments. Allergies are such a sensitive issue that if you do end up meeting someone who is sensitive and you have worn a scent that was too overpowering for them, you might not get the opportunity to see them again. And the sad thing is you will probably never know why.

Smelling fresh should be a given and this can be achieved by bathing frequently, using a good natural deodorant, and if you are going to wear a scent, play it safe by keeping it very light and to an absolute minimal amount.

The chemicals used in some of the commercial perfumes are so toxic that I personally choose not to wear them at all. If you have not already done so, check out the natural products at an aromatherapy store which offers a whole array of wonderful smelling natural scents for men and women. Not only do they smell wonderful but they are blended without the toxic chemicals you would find in some of the store bought products.

By going natural, not only will you smell good but you will also have the added benefits that aromatherapy products offer to help promote some form of either emotional or physical health. These products are also much more environmentally friendly. One more thing, always buy products that state they have not been tested on animals.

Clothes

When it comes to your wardrobe, my advice is to always dress appropriately for the occasion. If you are working you typically have your work wardrobe that may be required to abide by a certain dress code. You would then have a completely different set of clothes for going to the gym or participating in whatever sports you like, some nice clothes for going out for an evening, some casual clothes for your everyday life and perhaps some dressy casual clothes for when you go out shopping or to meet a friend or some other sort of social or public activity.

It often amazes me to see how so many people have all the different outfits to accommodate their various sports activities but when it comes to day to day attire, or even going out on a date, they simply don't have a clue.

The thing that will bring you down in the wardrobe department is having one style of clothes that you make do for any occasion. Here in Vancouver it seems that yoga pants have become somewhat of a permanent fashion statement, but in reality this is not the case. I have heard business managers complain about women showing up for a job interview wearing them, and men comment about them being worn out on a date. Realistically, would you ever consider wearing your soccer shorts or any other sort of fitness attire instead? Probably not, so remember yoga pants are for yoga and perhaps lounging around the house and that's about it.

You might feel that your clothes are not that important but they definitely can make a statement about you, your personality, and how you may live your life. You don't have to have the latest styles to get noticed but it is important to have a wardrobe that suits your personality and fits you well. Your clothes should also always be clean and in good repair.

Since we tend to have a very casual approach to dressing in North America, I believe that a large part of the population doesn't have a clue when it comes to dressing for a date. Therefore most people would do well to invest in a few hours with an image consultant as your image has a huge impact on every aspect of your life. And that includes dating, work or business. And just to prove my point here is a little piece of trivia I recently found in an article. A job offer could potentially bring up to 20% higher wages, to an applicant with a professional appearance. If that's not enough to get you motivated to smarten up, just think what your image is doing for your love life.

Shoes

Shoes say so much about your personality. Remember the saying: fashion is what you wear on your head and on your feet, everything else is merely an accessory. Shoes should fit well and be in good repair, and you must be able to walk properly in them.

Sneakers and gym shoes are just that. They should help you perform better in your fitness activities and make a statement only at the gym, but not on the street, in a business meeting or out on a date. The only statement that running shoes make in these situations is that you don't know how to put yourself together.

Guys, shoes are a good indication of your sense of style and confidence. But no matter what your taste or style in shoes, you need to keep them clean and scuff free, and also make sure that you take good care of the heels and soles. And remember no dark coloured socks with sandals!

Ladies, if you wear high heels, which I strongly recommend at least while out on a date, make sure you can walk in them. Men love high heel shoes as not only do they look sexy but they also impact the way a woman walks. However, if you don't know how to walk in them and end up waddling instead, you could end up looking more comical than attractive.

Keep your shoes in good repair by replacing the heel lifts as soon as they start to wear out, and be careful that your heels don't develop any cracks as they can split and cause you to fall. Just imagine how embarrassing that could be!

Strappy sandals and pointed toed stiletto heels are probably considered the most attractive and sexy shoes as they make the leg look slimmer and longer, and they also alter the way you look from both the back and side profiles. Chunky, clunky shoes tend to look more awkward. Think feminine: wearing a sexy pair of shoes can turn the most mundane outfit into a fun and flirtatious look and help you feel sexier, too.

Accessories

Accessories are a personal choice. They are meant to be fun and can help spruce up an outfit, but be careful not to go overboard. If your accessories are so overwhelming that admirers can't remember anything else about you, you might want to tone them down. Too many or over-sized accessories can be such a distraction that they may be the only thing that you are remembered for. Not such a great first impression to make.

If you really love the bigger bolder looks, keep the pieces to a minimum. If you are going to wear a chunky necklace then perhaps pair it off with a matching or similar bangle and that's it! I highly recommend that you don't add the rings and big dangling earrings to match.

Big fashion pieces are fun but smaller more dainty items are more feminine, elegant and sophisticated. Keep it simple, especially for casual occasions or for when you are going out on a first date.

Guys, watches, rings and pendants are great but again don't overdo it. Of course it depends on what statement you are trying to make. I have seen some guys who cannot give up wearing 3 o 4 silver skeleton and heavy metal rings which often give the impression that they are stuck in the heavy metal era or have a real rebellious side. If the rings are the only part of the outfit they wear, this tends to give the impression of immaturity. Again, keep it simple, don't overdo it and when it comes to accessories, the golden rule is this, dress appropriately for the occasion.

Making a first impression is paramount and even if you feel that you are not in the best shape or not where you want to be in life, at least make the effort to be the very best that you can be for now. Personal development and creating a new image incorporates both long and short term goals, and it is much easier to motivate yourself to achieve your long term goals if you feel good about yourself now.

Chapter 9

How To Use Your Body Language To Build Rapport

Have you ever wondered what it would be like to be able to read people? Believe it or not it is not that difficult. You can learn so much about a person by the way he or she moves, interacts with others or even by their eye movements. Considering our body language has such a huge impact on how others see us and interpret who they think we are, maybe we had better be careful about what we are saying with it.

Now imagine what might happen if you *could* read people. What sort of impact do you think that having this ability would have on building rapport and developing relationships? In reality, we all do a pretty good job of reading each other although for the most part it is something we do unconsciously. However, if we were able to become more aware, and understand each other's states and body language it would certainly give us an advantage on how we could develop relationships and build rapport.

If you take a good look around, you will see that people come in all shapes, sizes, colors, and from different social backgrounds, and yet perhaps what makes each and every one of us so interesting and unique is the way in which we behave. It is our mannerisms, body language and personality which truly set us apart. And even though these traits may not actually be of the physical nature, they are largely responsible for how people see each other.

Think about people you may know or have seen when they are in different frames of mind, or different emotional states. Even for a temporary state of sadness or depression a person's physiology will change. He or she will likely be somewhat cowered in posture and their eyes will probably be cast down. Their breathing may be more shallow and their movements slower.

People in this state are also usually much slower to respond, and their physical energy is depleted.

Then there is the angry person who walks around all pent up with shoulders pulled up towards their ears, clenched fists and a tight jaw. Breathing may be more rapid and everything is tight, so much so that they may also be rubbing their neck or temples to ease the tension caused by their hunched and tense posture. They usually walk faster and tend to be very focused on what they are doing. It is as if they have a mission even if it is only to spoil someone else's day. There will likely be a lot of emphasis in the body movements, especially flailing arms as if their purpose is to get other people's attention, and they have a tendency to make others feel very uncomfortable.

People who are nervous or shy tend to look as though they are weary and wish to disappear into the background, and they may even take on some of the characteristics or traits of a sad or angry person. Fear causes them to breathe shallow or possibly even hyperventilate. They may be pale due to the oxygen imbalance and may even physically shake.

Then, on the other side of the spectrum there is the social butterfly who scoots around looking to see who they can talk to. Usually bright-eyed and very aware, although perhaps somewhat distracted, they don't miss an opportunity to stop for a chat. These people who are generally happy have good skin tone and color. They also breathe more deeply and look more relaxed in everything they do. They have good energy, both physical and magnetic and people are naturally drawn to them because for the most part, these people make us feel good.

A confident person will stand tall no matter how tall they actually are, and often have what is considered to be good posture. Shoulders will be pulled back but down, chest out, tummy pulled in and hands relaxed. When standing, they may shift their weight to one leg and perhaps even place one of their hands on their hip. When gesturing with their hands their palms and thumbs will usually be more exposed. They make good eye contact, smile a lot and just look comfortable with themselves in general.

These are just a few of the examples of states that people spend their time in, and the physical signs associated with these states show the world how we are feeling and what is going on with us. Depending on what state a person is in will determine how approachable they appear to the rest of the world. As I have already mentioned, although we are not always conscious of it we are all experts at reading each other's body language, and we get feelings or pick up vibes partly based on what we see. I'm sure you can now see that people really are quite easy to read.

Now that you are perhaps a little more aware of these states and how they are seen by others, perhaps it would be good practice to go out and people watch to see if you can determine what states you can recognize. Then try some of the states on for yourself, it's kind of like walking in another person's shoes. To do this all you have to do is shift your body into the same posture as a person in a particular state, and include the same eye and breathing patterns so that you can really experience how it feels to be them.

Practice with positive states to start, and then if you are going to test out some negative states only try them for a few minutes at most making sure that you get back into a positive state again afterwards.

Then, take a really good look around you to scout out people who you think are in the states that you would like to be in. Focus on people who are happy, outgoing and confident. Watch to see exactly what state they are in and what they do. Observe their body language and pay attention to how they stand, move and interact with others. Then observe to see what results they get from their interactions. I find people watching very fascinating as I love to watch how people interact with others and notice the outcomes they get.

Learn which states are positive and try them on for yourself, practicing on a daily basis. By doing so you can literally integrate these behaviours into your mind/body system and these states will become locked in at a cellular level. Don't get into the habit of doing this with negative states as the same thing applies to them too. Just remember people aren't typically born angry or nasty, but develop these behaviours over time. This is a very valuable tool as we can learn, and practice to become anything we want. And that includes becoming a happy, confident person.

Building Rapport

Think about this for a moment. Have you ever noticed how with some people, even though you may have just met, you feel as though you have known each other for years? It may even feel as though you are like old friends. Have you ever wondered why this happens? The answer very often has a lot to do with rapport.

The reason we typically click and like someone is because by nature we like people who are like ourselves. We are comfortable around people who speak our lingo, see things the way we see them, or feel the way we feel. I am not talking about languages per se; I am actually talking about living in, and communicating in the same sensory world as we do.

Good communicators have the ability to build rapport with most people. However, if you meet someone who tends to mismatch or who just doesn't treat you right, this can be a real problem to overcome. But typically you can build rapport by understanding how a person experiences the world and then match them at their level, or as they would say in NLP, meet them in their model of the World. You can also build rapport by using similar body language and using the same verbal preferences.

To keep it simple, consider the fact that we take everything in through our six senses. The information gets filtered and then we communicate it back to the world using our own preferred senses by which we prefer to live by. For example:

Visual

People who are visual prefer to experience the world though their eyes, or through their mind's eye. When they explain a day at the beach it might sound something like.

Oh it was such a <u>beautiful place</u>. The sun was <u>shining on the water</u>, it was <u>so pretty</u> and <u>I watched</u> the birds gliding in the wind with <u>the sun glistening</u> on their wings. In the distance <u>I could see a ship</u>.

When explaining something to a visual person they might say - <u>I see your point!</u>

Visual people use descriptive words based on what they see.

Visual people tend to be very upright in stance and keep a bit more of a distance from who they are talking too as they like to be able to observe and take in the whole picture.

Auditory

An auditory person may describe their day at the beach more like this. What a great day the <u>wind just screamed</u> and howled around and the seagulls were <u>squawking</u>. The children were all <u>laughing and giggling</u> and I could even <u>hear the ship blowing its horn.</u>

If you explain something to an auditory person he may respond with… <u>I hear you!</u> Or Hmm, <u>that rings a bell</u>!

Auditory people describe things by what they hear.

Auditory people may not be that great at making eye contact when talking with you as they are concentrating on what they hear. To do a better job at listening they may look down, as not to get distracted by what they see. They may also tilt their head to the side a bit so that they can hear well. They may even cradle their chin in between their thumb and index finger.

Kinaesthetic

Kinaesthetic people are the more touchy feely type. You will often hear people describe a kinaesthetic person by saying just that, you know he is the touchy feely type. Or hear comments such as, you can't be all touchy feely in business.

The kinaesthetic person would describe a day at the beach in the following manner. <u>Oh it felt great</u>, I was <u>so relaxed</u>. The sun and sand <u>felt</u> so warm and the <u>breeze blew softly soothing</u> my sun burnt skin. The <u>water felt cold</u> though!

When conversing with a kinaesthetic person you will hear them say, <u>I feel that</u> this is the way to go, or <u>I have a bad feeling</u> about that.

A kinaesthetic person will tend to stand closer to you than others who use the preceding sensory systems as they like to feel your energy and they also like to touch. They will be the ones who will rub your arm when you look a little dismayed or give you a hug when they see you. Kinaesthetic people describe things by how they feel about them.

These are the three systems that we want to become particularly aware of when it comes to meeting people, making friends, building rapport and developing relationships. Even though olfactory and gustatory are the other two senses we would have learned about in school, it is highly unlikely that you will meet too many people who are olfactory, gustatory communicators.

We do however all use all of our senses all of the time. And as for the sixth sense, although not that well understood by many, it is likely the most important sense when it comes to finding that chemistry which we all crave. But, that will be a whole other book.

The point of knowing this information is because when we identify which sensory system a person primarily operates in, we can shift into their preferred system to build rapport and gain more trust.

This is what communication between people operating in different sensory systems may sound like.

"Hey Laddie, I went to the beach last night, it was great, I saw the kids playing and the sun setting down on the ocean." Mr. Auditory may respond by saying, "yes I was there, did you hear that raucous of a noise they called a band?" Ms. Visual says, "didn't see that!"

Can you see or hear how the communication between the two gets a bit fragmented? It is almost as if they are speaking in two different languages here.

Now, you can probably see where communication friction comes in.

So as I mentioned earlier, we like people who are like ourselves. They don't have to look like us or agree with us, but we do however like them to communicate and behave in a manner similar to ours. By learning to recognize and use these communication styles, we can bridge communication gaps and build better rapport with more people. These people will be more likely to like and trust you and they won't even think about it, or know why. It can be our little secret!

Now would be a good time to practice building these skills, so I suggest that you go and find someone to talk to. Ask them some random questions and see if you can figure out what sensory systems they prefer using. If you are not sure to start with, ask questions that require the person to describe something to you, such as a day at the beach, and then listen carefully to the words they use.

In my opinion, learning to recognize the differences people have, and the way we all do things differently, should be used solely for the purpose of seeing the person's individuality and unique qualities. Problems happen when one or both people are very opinionated or judgmental and see these differences as being wrong because others do not match their own perceptions, based on their own individual experiences. We need to recognize and appreciate these differences between people in order to build real trust and rapport.

Detailed vs. Big Picture.

Another thing that we can drive each other crazy over is the amount of detail that we use in our vocabulary. Some people see the big picture while others focus on the individual details.

A good example of this would be, if someone was to ask me where Richmond is, I would probably point across the water and say, it's over there! I am primarily a big picture person.

You could then ask someone else the same question and they would give you a very detailed reply, explaining every single step of the way. They would point you in the right direction, draw you a map and give you a blow-by-blow run down of each little detail or landmark to watch out for including where their aunt's sister's nephew's brother's friend lives.

When it comes to communicating in general this is one way people can drive each other nuts. If I am asking a question that warrants a yes or no answer, that is exactly what I want to hear, yes, or no! I don't need to know the history of how you come to that yes or no answer which takes fifteen minutes to explain. A very detailed person would hate the yes or no answer as there just wouldn't be enough information or detail for them to make sense of it.

To be effective and a good communicator you will need to be aware of other people's patterns and to know how to communicate at both ends of this spectrum. Depending on what we are trying to achieve will determine which communication style would be most effective. For instance, if you want to build a house, then the picture which you have in your mind of that particular house would be the big picture. However, in order to draw out the plan and give someone instructions to build it, you will need to break the idea down into smaller chunks and put the details down on paper in order to bring it to life.

Just be aware of these communication styles and do your best to match whichever communication style the person with whom you are talking to is using. Otherwise, you could drive each other crazy and end relationships over this stuff. These communication styles have way more impact in our lives than we would ever care to admit. So remember that good communicators learn to recognize body language and the different styles of communication. And then they automatically use them to match and build rapport with whoever they are talking to.

Mirroring

Another way to build rapport is by using a method called mirroring. Very different from mimicking, mirroring in a respectful way represents likeness and is an excellent way to build rapport. It is something that good communicators do naturally and we do so by observing the subtle changes and movements in another person's body language, then match or cross match what they are doing. Depending on how skilled you are at this, you can learn to observe eye and breathing patters, notice changes in breathing rates and skin color and watch for subtle shifts in posture or body movement.

For our purpose I suggest you learn to observe and mirror posture, body movements and breathing patterns.

In order to mirror breathing patterns I would suggest you try to find someone who is willing to practice with you, if not, just take yourself down to a coffee shop or somewhere where you and the people that you will be observing will be seated. Start by relaxing and pay attention to your own breathing patterns. Try to take slow, deep breaths, but do not emphasize your breathing to the extent that others will necessarily notice what you are doing. Try to get into a bit of a meditative or at least relaxed state.

Then select someone to observe, preferably someone who is sitting alone and maybe reading a book. It is easier if they are sitting upright or back in their chair as opposed to slumped over a table. Watch to see if they are breathing through their mouth or through their nose. Then watch their shoulders and upper chest area to see if you can pick up on their breathing patterns. The easiest type of candidate to observe for this exercise would be a sleeping baby, so if you do happen to see one, go for it.

Then slowly and gently mirror their breathing pattern. Look for depth and rate of breath. If they are breathing very shallow or hyperventilating you might not want to mirror them as you could end up feeling dizzy or stressed. Watch out for a sigh or a stretch, as these are also good movements to mirror too. Practice on several people to see if you feel the difference from one person to the next, and see if you feel more in harmony with anyone in particular.

When you have mastered the art of mirroring, you can pace the process for a while and then change the pace so that you lead the other person to follow and mirror you.

A good time to do this would be when you are talking to someone who is really wound up or stressed out. You could start by mirroring them, although maybe to a slightly lesser degree, as this builds rapport because you are now alike. Then gradually calm down, take deeper breaths and lead them into a more relaxed state, it is probable that they will naturally and unconsciously follow you.

The next thing to mirror is a person's posture. If you are talking to someone who is leaning to one side, you might want to assume a similar (but not identical) posture. For instance, you could be joining someone for a business meeting. Your guest walks in and sits bolt upright, and you will probably straighten up pretty quick. We are all used to doing this when in the presence of an authoritative figure. But we can do the same in reverse, when appropriate.

If you meet or are sitting across from someone who is slouched with one elbow on the table and their chin resting in their hand, you could mirror them by leaning in a similar manner. Perhaps you could lean with your temple or cheekbone resting on your hand, or, you could lean back in your chair but leaning off to the side a bit so that you are sitting at an angle similar to them. This creates an automatic sense of acceptance and likeness. We like people who are like ourselves, remember?

And, finally, movement is a good thing to mirror. You could be sitting close to someone who is tapping their pen on the table or rocking a bit in the chair to the rhythm of music, so you could mirror them by crossing your legs and swinging your foot or tapping it on the floor to the same beat that they are tapping their pen. As I mentioned earlier, this is really easy to do, you just need to practice the process a bit. By doing so, it will help you to build rapport with someone and will ultimately put you in a position to then, after they unconsciously trust you, to lead them into another level of communication, if this is what you want.

Space proximity

Finally, when it comes to building rapport you need to be aware of and respect other people's space. Everyone, depending on their culture, their beliefs and their sensory preference will have different requirements for how much space they like around themselves, and how comfortable they are with you invading their space.

The typical distance you need to be aware of with a relative stranger or acquaintance is between about four and twelve feet. If you want to move in closer you need to closely observe their body language. If they move back or turn away from you a bit as you approach, then you might want to back off a bit.

If in the company of someone with whom you are really friendly or if you are attracted to each other, you are permitted to move in closer and could probably enter into the six to eighteen inch range. If you are friends but are not considered intimate (as in family, close friend or lover) you will need to give the person between around eighteen inches and four feet.

People generally like more space in front of them than at their sides or behind them. If you want to get closer to a man then a side approach would be the way to go, but if you want to approach a woman, you should do so face on.

Again, you need to be aware of the other person's body language. People are very protective of their personal space, and to invade it is almost as intrusive as to physically step on them.

The key to building rapport is about reading the other person's body language, facial expressions and energy and then gently respond to what you see, hear and feel.

Chapter 10

To Become A Fun Loving Dynamic Free Spirit You Need To Flirt

Be A Flirt

F Fun, Friendly, Funny, Fabulous

L Laughter, Loving, Light Hearted, Lusty

I Irresistible, Imaginative, Igniting, Intriguing

R Romantic, Rebellious, Refreshing, Ravishing

T Tempting, Teasing, Tremendous, Toying, Touch

What Do The Words Flirt and Flirting Mean To You?

Depending on where in the world you're from and what you have been raised to believe, your ideas of what a flirt is, or what it means to flirt would very likely be significantly different from someone of a different culture.

Beliefs about flirting tend to be attached to our identity, meaning that if you believe that flirting is an acceptable and fun act you will likely be considered a fun and friendly person if you flirt. Or, if you have been raised to believe that flirting is too forward or even promiscuous, you may have feelings of shame or embarrassment attached to the idea of being a flirt. Either way, whatever your belief, it is likely that it will have a significant impact on if or how you allow yourself to flirt.

Unfortunately for many the idea of flirting has been met with some resistance and often great disapproval. And, because of these strong beliefs that have been passed down through time or throughout cultures as the case might be, some people are actually really quite confused about what flirting is really all about. And perhaps because of these beliefs have chosen not to participate in flirting at all.

Hmmm… there must be some real misconceptions about flirting for this to happen. However, flirting is actually a natural way of being, it is the negative beliefs that we have become bound by which prevent us from being happy and expressive people that is not so natural at all.

Flirting is inspired and initiated by a basic human instinct. We flirt when the playful side of our personality gets the urge to let loose and throws caution to the wind. If we decide to go for it and participate in a good flirting session, we can have a lot of fun. But, if on the other hand we constantly refrain from engaging in this level of social interaction, we might end up with a life time of missed connections and regretful disappointments.

Flirting is the key to opening the door to new opportunities. But sadly it is something that so many people find terribly uncomfortable to do. It is as if the urge is there but our analytical brain steps in causing us to hesitate and over evaluate a situation instead of just taking action. It seems that many of us have trained ourselves to refrain from expressing ourselves in front of others, and in the process we hold back and suppress our feelings and desires.

The sad thing is that if you are someone who doesn't flirt, you are far more likely to miss out on meeting new friends, connecting with great people, building good friendships, and sadly losing out on the opportunity to meet that one special person who might have been the love of your life.

Changing The Face Of Flirting

Flirting is something that we do to set our spirits free, and in turn we can bring out the best in those we flirt with. Flirting is a very natural and instinctive way to communicate and interact with others, and it is a great way to make new contacts and develop new friendships.

There are of course many levels of flirting, and depending on what your intentions are will determine what style of flirting you will choose to engage in. For the purpose of initiating a friendly or social encounter we should focus primarily on flirting for fun, to build rapport and develop a level of communication. If it is a romantic connection that you are looking for then you need to turn it up a notch in order to send out the signals that you want to connect outside of the buddy, buddy or "let's be friends" realm.

Flirting is also a great way to build closer relationships. The more we flirt with people we like, the more fun we will have enjoying each other's company and in turn we will automatically become more comfortable around each other.

We flirt with people to make them feel good, and if they respond favourably it makes us feel good too. Flirting is a bit of a game, and if our opponent chooses to play along, a sense of familiarity sets in and bridges the gap to new friendships in mere moments. It is human nature to flirt, and when done in the right way and in the right situations, flirting can ignite romantic affairs.

It is as if something magical happens when people flirt and the only rules to the game are that you accept each other on a level that says… you're ok, just be yourself, you can let your guard down and drop all the formalities, relax, have fun, be friends and enjoy each other's company.

Flirting is respectful fun and playful interaction. We flirt in an effort to both give and attract attention with a mutual goal to build a warm and friendly rapport. It is where we allow ourselves to smile, pay compliments to each other and joke around with playful banter in the hopes that we will bring out the best in those we interact with. Flirting is a contact sport, and in my mind it is the most natural art of being truly human.

We can and do flirt with people of all ages and from many walks of life. And, perhaps without even realizing it, we may be flirting with people all day long.

We flirt with our friends, our families, children and the elderly, and some of us may even flirt with pets. As long as you are happy, cheery, charming and sociable, you may be an excellent flirt already even though you may not have been aware that you were flirting at all.

Where In The World Can We Find The Best Flirts?

Many cultures nurture natural flirts, and when in their presence as long as we are comfortable to receive their attention we are likely to join in and flirt right back with them too. We may think of these people as being warm, friendly and expressive, but whichever way we look at it they are experts at what they do. People who flirt know the art of being social human beings.

People from places like Mexico and South or Central America are brilliant flirts. These people tend to live life with passion, and they are not afraid to express themselves. They also tend to really live in their bodies and not just in their heads, and are very often kinaesthetic and touchy feely types by nature.

These people make great eye contact, connect, smile and seem to be so warm and friendly. They love to dance and sing and we often find them captivating as they lure us into their fun-loving ways. They are social and are known to celebrate every opportunity they can.

In these cultures everybody flirts, the men, the women, the young and the old and we even see these qualities and behaviours in very young children. This is no surprise really when you consider the fact that it is part of their nature.

While in Mexico we were overwhelmed with all the attention we were getting from the local men. It didn't matter if they were waiters, bus drivers, cabbies or professionals. And as for expressive, we even had a waiter sing to us, translating his favourite Spanish love songs. And as he sang his body language and facial expressions were to die for.

As the young waiter's friends joined in, even though they were probably all teens or in their early twenties at most, they were telling us how much they love romance, and how they love to be in love. The people of this culture are definitely not afraid to share how they feel.

Europeans are also wonderful flirts. They greet each other, touch more often by hugging, kissing each other on the cheek, holding hands, walking arm in arm and using more expressive and alluring body language.

European's also tend to live in their bodies and not just in their heads. They take pride in their appearance and have less hang ups over looks. They seem to be very connected with each other intellectually as well as physically, more so than some other cultures. They also seem to have their priorities right when it comes to people as they devote a great deal of their time to family and friends.

Europeans spend a lot of time eating, drinking and celebrating life with company. They are curious about each other's lives and like to focus their attention on each other as opposed to themselves, asking more questions and listening to stories, laughing, reminiscing and enjoying each other's company.

Brits are also great flirts, mostly because they are typically more open to talk too just about anyone. Their social habits, which often revolve around pubs and dinner parties, encourage social interaction, and they also use humour which is always good for breaking the ice, having a laugh and building rapport.

Talking to, and reading internet dating profiles of people from different parts of the world, I found that in the UK people are still far more interested in personality, good company and getting together with someone for a laugh, than they are in looks. Perhaps it is because of this attitude that they don't seem to be so hung up on their own insecurities as they rely more on their personality, sense of humour and banter to connect with people. This seems to be a major difference compared to the North American culture.

In all of the countries mentioned above it seems that a man who doesn't necessarily have a lot going for him would still put himself out there to approach and flirt with a beautiful woman.

In North America we are not necessarily so good at the flirting thing. We look but don't touch, we glance but look away quickly pretending that we never even noticed the person that we found attractive and we have a tendency to turn our opposite sex friends into just that, friends, and if the connection is there, friends with benefits, at best. We see people that we want to approach but just can't bring ourselves around to making that contact and when we do, we are not necessarily very good at expressing ourselves in a way that shows we are interested in them or want to be more than just friends.

I do realize that this behaviour is not just a North American phenomenon; however it is one that seems to be experienced by so many singles in this part of the world. And it opens up the question as to why.

Why is it that we have such a hard time making the connection? Loneliness is a terrible thing and the one thing that humans crave more than anything is true love, and yet we hold back, deny our needs, refrain from connecting, and consequently suffer in silence.

Why do so many people feel that isolated that they have come to the conclusion that they will never find that one special person who they would love to share their life with? Whatever happened to the dream of happily ever after? When perhaps all it would take to start the ball rolling is a friendly acknowledgment of an attractive stranger, a reciprocated smile and a simple hello.

With too many theories to speculate on, some of the common beliefs include the fact that we are so politically correct that we are afraid of offending people, and that we are so used to instant gratification and filling our lives with material things that we are always looking for the next best thing. And maybe without realizing it, we even do this very same thing with people. For whatever the reason one of the symptoms of our behaviour is that we in North America have become so dependent on internet dating that many of us have lost the art of natural connection. And, when we do date we practice a form of dating that often seems "tentative" at best.

In an attempt to find out why so many people have a problem with the simple acts of making eye contact, smiling, talking to each other and flirting, I spoke with and listened to the concerns that so many single people were willing to share. This was what I found.

While working as a stylist in Vancouver, BC I had the opportunity to meet and chat with hundreds of people from all over the globe. Many who now reside in this part of the world expressed their difficulties of being single, and the challenges they have experienced when trying to meet, connect with, and develop relationships in this part of the world.

Women are asking, what is wrong with the men here? Why do they not pursue us? And why are they not asking us out? And the men are expressing their own frustrations, in particular with how difficult they find it to approach a woman without getting ignored or shot down. And everyone was asking, where should one go to meet Mr. or Miss. Right?

Intrigued by this sad state of affairs I started to pay more attention, ask more questions, observe more interactions and even organized social gatherings for singles, and come up with some of the suggestions and possible solutions that I share in my books. And I'll share a little of what "he said she said" to shed some light on what might be at the root of some of these problems.

Through a combination of speaking with singles, and online questionnaires I found that men had three major concerns. The first was that many men told me that they had been shot down so bad when approaching a woman that they just wouldn't put themselves through that again. The second was that a lot of men expressed that they no longer know what women actually want. And the third was that most men I spoke with said they were just too shy, and to be honest with you under most circumstances these days, I can understand why.

Many of the women on the other hand expressed that men are just not pursuing, making an effort or doing anything to make them feel special. Some women even shared their experiences of the lack of respect that they would expect to receive from a man that was supposed to be interested in them. And, many complained about how a lot of men that they met, expected the woman do all the running around to meet him, and when going out on a date, to often even pick up the tab.

From many of the stories and experiences that I heard there seemed to be a definite sense of disconnect between men and women, and instead of flirting it seemed to be more like a battle between the sexes than a pursuit of friendship or love. Hearing these stories it was not hard to see why men found it difficult to approach women and that women were feeling neglected.

Perhaps some of the main differences when it comes to dating between the North American and the European or South American cultures has to do with expectations and effort.

In places such as Europe, where you see a lot more flirting between men and women it seems that there is simply a greater appreciation and acceptance for this type of interaction. It also appears that men and women simply seem to have a greater level of respect and admiration for each other, and there may still be more of a distinction between gender roles. Women living in these regions typically expect to be admired and pursued by a man, and the men expect to do the pursuing and enjoy the chase.

If we look at expectations within different cultures, we can start to see the patterns and the cause and effect of our own beliefs and behaviours. And by doing so we may develop a better understanding of why we are having such a problem in this area of our lives. When men are saying they will not approach women because of the way they are treated, perhaps it is because they are getting a very different response from these women than what their European and Southern counterparts might receive.

A European man may think that if he pays attention to a woman she will be flattered, this makes him look good and he feels more like a man. If a North American man thinks that if he pays attention to a woman he will get shot down or threatened with a law suit, then he worries about looking like an idiot and he feels even more insecure. It is human nature that our expectation is to get more of the same, for the man who gets shot down, why would he want to put himself through that again? However, if he never tries because he is simply too shy or because of what he has read or heard, then his lack of effort will get him nowhere.

Yikes…. This topic often seems more like the battle of the sexes than a pursuit to find true love and happiness.

I hate to say it, and of course this does not apply to everyone as there are plenty of people who are dating, having good relationships, being nice to each other and who are secure with themselves and are great flirts, but we do have a bit of an issue with flirting in this part of the world. And from what I have seen and heard, if we don't start to pay attention to what works, and start taking some tips from the cultures that are good at flirting, and start practicing some of their techniques, we may not get to enjoy the rewards of attracting fun and fabulous people into our lives.

How Does It Feel When Someone Flirts With You?

Think for a moment about a time when someone noticed you and did a double take. You just knew that they liked what they saw. So how did it make you feel? What crossed your mind at the time? I'm sure you felt at least a little bit flattered. Without realizing it, you probably straightened up your posture, pulled your shoulders back and felt a little bit of a rush. You might have even been so flattered that you had to fight back that smile of yours from beaming from ear to ear.

Then try to remember a specific time when someone paid you a really nice compliment. It may have been about anything from the way you looked or something that you said or did. How did you feel? Were you comfortable with that, or did you try to divert the attention away from yourself by changing the subject or causing some other kind of distraction? Even if you weren't completely comfortable with the idea, I bet the incident crossed your mind again later and you possibly wondered about that person who made you feel good.

Or how do you feel when you are around a person who simply gives you a little extra attention? It's nice to know that people notice us and think we are special.

I know that sometimes if we are not used to getting attention or if we have been taught that flirting or even being friendly is thought of as being too forward or aggressive, and has been disapproved of by someone you respect, it can feel uncomfortable to receive the attention. But, let's face it, it is nice when someone takes notice of us.

Most of us love to get noticed, receive compliments and be flattered by anyone, never mind someone of the opposite sex or someone who we find attractive. It makes us feel good even if we try to hide it. So why would we not want to go around making other people feel good too?

Another question, how do you feel when you see someone who is really outgoing and everyone is drawn or attracted to them? How does that make you feel? Do you wish you could be a little more like them, or does it make you feel dislike towards them for being so popular or liked?

If you find that the latter is true for you, it is not that uncommon a response. The truth is that very often when we find we don't like something about another person it is usually a reflection of the very thing that we don't like about ourselves. As in, if we don't like someone to be so outgoing and friendly, it is often because we are a little jealous and wish that we could be a bit more like them. The problem is that when this happens and we feel this way, we may defend our position and therefore resist change.

By becoming aware of our thoughts and feelings, and by challenging our beliefs, we may arrive at a place of awareness that will ultimately allow us to facilitate change.

We can all become good flirts and we certainly don't have to wait for others to flirt with us first. What's to stop you from spending your day going around cheering people up and making them feel good? If you are not so comfortable receiving attention you can still be a great flirt by putting the attention on them and not making it all about you. Being friendly and flirting is a natural way of being, not expressing ourselves and suppressing our feelings is not, because it is the latter that is the learned behaviour. So go ahead and flirt a little, the results could be extremely rewarding.

Who Can We Practice Our Flirting Techniques With?

You can flirt with absolutely anyone. You just have to think about what message you want to get across and then act accordingly. Just remember for the sake of building confidence we are talking about light hearted friendly flirting.

Since flirting is about making others feel good I think elderly people are often really good fun to flirt with, and they usually enjoy it too. A lot of seniors feel a bit invisible and yet they love the company and are usually up for a bit of a laugh. As long as you are being respectful and flirting in a positive, friendly and complimentary manner it is usually very well accepted. It is appreciated by seniors to receive comments or compliments that will help them feel young again, or make them feel valuable, attractive or loved. So a good statement or witty banter that will make them feel good will often go down well.

Just make sure that you spend a bit of time building rapport before you get too familiar with people, and so that you can determine whether or not that particular person is going to appreciate a little extra attention.

You don't want to cross any boundaries or offend anyone, so watch for signals from body language and facial expressions of the person that you are flirting with. If they are having fun and enjoying the interaction, then go for it.

When we flirt with strangers we are often just trying to build rapport and make their day a little bit brighter. I'm talking more about the people who perhaps work in your local coffee shop or grocery store. You get to see them on a regular basis so you might as well enjoy your time together. They'll soon remember you and look forward to seeing and serving you again. Ever wonder why some people get better treatment than others? Well there's your answer.

Flirting with strangers can be easily done, you need do nothing more than cross the line into being a little extra friendly, acknowledging them, smiling, sharing a little joke and perhaps a wink to let them know you are kidding around. Most people, no matter who they are, love this, and they will remember you as a very friendly person and will look forward to seeing you again. If people like you, they will go out of their way for you.

Babies are good flirts. If you flirt with them, they will flirt right back at you. When you make eye contact with a baby they will send you a big beaming smile and may even start to chuckle if you smile back. Mums often comment on what a flirt their child is and as long as you are not intruding or crossing any boundaries most people are flattered that you have noticed, and want to give their baby or child a little bit of attention. If you are going to go gaga over a baby, make sure that you build rapport with the parent first by asking them a couple of questions about their baby, or ask if it is ok for you to see their baby before making your approach. And, only ever flirt or kid around with young children if their parents are right there with them and you have made eye contact with them and received a smile of approval.

As I mentioned, we flirt with pets, giving them lots of attention and baby talk too, and they absolutely love us to death for it. And, it's a great way to flirt with their owners a bit in the process, if appropriate.

Gay men are awesome flirts and because of their warm and friendly demeanour we love them for it. I love going into restaurants, coffee shops or stores where I know some of these people work because I love the way they make me feel special, and enjoy the fact that we can have a bit of fun at the same time. And just for the record I've never met a woman to this day who wouldn't agree that we all love gay men. So there you go guys, if you flirt with us we are going to love you for it too, so stop being so shy and get out there and flirt!

Ladies, we have to become good flirts to let guys know where they stand. When we flirt we give these guys the green light to approach and perhaps even a little boost of confidence to help them along their way. So as you can see we can flirt with practically anyone and everyone, within reason. Flirting is just friendly interaction, to do so doesn't mean that you have to take them home or marry them.

Who Not To Flirt With

All this flirting is a lot of fun, but do use a little discretion for the sake of safety, respect for others and perhaps your job.

Know the difference between flirting and being a tease. One can get you in an awful lot of trouble while the other is more about being an outgoing and fun loving person. Never flirt with a drunk, someone on drugs or anyone who may be unpredictable. And of course we all have certain types of people that we do not want to attract or encourage into our lives, so we definitely don't want to be flirting with them either.

It's probably not a good idea to flirt with your boss or with professional clients as you are likely to soon lose credibility and any respect from them and your coworkers. And, never flirt with your friend's husband or wife unless you all know each other well enough to pull it off while having a bit of fun with it. Ok, ok you do have to use a bit of discretion. But have some fun, and always be safe.

How To Evolve Into A Super Friendly Flirt

There are many ways in which to flirt and depending on what you are trying to achieve, and who you are flirting with, will determine the style of flirting you would employ. Perhaps some of the most important things to be aware of when you set out to become a great flirt are, first, you need to remember that there is a time and a place for everything, and secondly, you need to pay close attention to reading the body language of the person with whom you are flirting. By doing so you can gauge your interactions and act accordingly, flirting is after all about building rapport.

When we are attracted to someone, whether we know them or not we need to give them a sign so that they will get the hint that we are interested. By doing so we are giving them the signal that says, I kind of like you, or at least what I see, and yes, I am giving you permission to approach and pursue, or I'd like to approach you. If nothing else by flirting with them you are going to make that person feel good, and remember what makes someone a super attractive person? It is how they make us feel when we are around them, and vice versa. Are you starting to get how this works now?

When we flirt with people we already know, we do it in a very playful and fun-loving way. People who are comfortable with this sort of attention will often tease each other, joke around, touch each other on the hand or arm, or perhaps pat each other on the back or shoulder, or even gently touch an opponent's face while playfully commenting on a personal joke.

If there are other people present, the one doing the teasing may wink at onlookers as if to include them and let them in on the game. We often see this type of behaviour with people who know each other well, such as close friends, family members or anyone that they feel close enough with to act this way around.

Flirting To See If There Is A Mutual Attraction

Very often we may find ourselves in a situation where we have an encounter with a complete stranger who we happen to find attractive. This may be a situation where we spot someone in the check-out line of a grocery store, or walking past us on the street. Situations like this happen more often than not and when they do we need to act fast as we may have only seconds or at best minutes in which to capture their attention and send out some sort of signal to let them know that we like what we see, and that we are in fact interested in them.

In these situations, since time is of the essence, you need to be able to jump right into flirt mode. The chances are you have already made eye contact and if you have looked away you will definitely have to look back. Then, holding your eye contact for a little longer, you will need to add in a smile. If you are shy that is fine; you just look away for a second to break the intensity, take a deep breath and then look back again. If you are both interacting with each other in this way then you can be pretty certain that they are interested in you too.

You also need to use body language. If you are standing, straighten up and turn your body towards the person you are attracted to. If you are walking by, turn your head towards them and smile as the two of you pass by. Now would be a good time to say something, then slow down, look back and smile again.

If you're not sure what to say, just say hello and ask how they are doing-that's a good start. Otherwise, how about saying the first thing that comes into your head? What have you got to lose, other than the opportunity to connect with that person, if you *don't* flirt with them? In a nutshell, the only way to make that instant connection is to flirt.

Be prepared for the next time that you have an encounter with an attractive stranger. Think about what you would like to say? Rehearse some lines that you would feel comfortable using in a situation where you would like to start a conversation with an attractive stranger, and then visualize yourself doing it.

How To Flirt With Someone You Fancy

Now that we can see how easy and natural it is to flirt, let's take a little closer look at what it means to, and how to, flirt with someone that we know and find attractive.

If the person you are attracted to is actually, say a friend or an acquaintance, but you are not sure if they feel or think about you in the same way, playful flirting might actually be what is needed to plant that idea into their mind. You need to be a little more flirty playful than buddy, buddy. Use more eye contact, move in on the other person's personal space to see how they respond, and perhaps even joke around the idea of "if we were dating, or kissing, or….." And then watch out and notice any positive responses.

If they pick up on your actions they may start to think, hmm, maybe there is more to this than meets the eye, and who knows the idea just might ignite something in their mind. If they respond favourably, then by all means continue with the flirting. If they look at you a bit strange, then you can always use the… "just joking" line.

If the playful element doesn't work because perhaps you know each other on more of a serious note, or you are just too shy, then you might have to show your vulnerabilities. We all inherently know that people can be really shy when they are around someone they are attracted too. If you are shy when you are in the company of someone that you are particularly fond of, this alone might be enough to give them a bit of a hint about how you feel about them. Don't try to hide this vulnerability because if you don't give off some kind of a message to let the other person know how you feel about them then how will they ever know what you are thinking?

Simple Flirting Tips

For Random Scenarios

Flirting In A Grocery Store

Grocery stores are great places to practice your flirting techniques. There are tons of single people meandering, checking out what and perhaps *who* they would like to have for dinner. First saunter by to see what they have in their basket. Single items and small portions are a dead giveaway that they are cooking for one.

If you are feeling gutsy, you could walk up to someone with a side dish that would go well with that chicken portion they have in their basket. While looking into their basket you could suggest something to the effect that their chicken was meant to be coupled with the rice or whatever it is that you are holding in your hand. Then, make eye contact, smile and suggest in your own personal style, that you could put your theory to the test by making dinner together.

If they say yes, run home, clean up, get a bottle of wine and make sure that you make a great and lasting impression.

Flirting On A Bus

As you get onto the bus, do a quick scan to see if there is anyone of great interest. If not, just pick someone you can just practice this with. Then try to sit somewhere that you know you can't be missed by that person whose attention you want to grab. Make frequent eye contact, and from time to time a brief smile. Then as you move to leave the bus, walk away from them, then stop, turn back, make eye contact and flash a great big smile before you leave. I can almost guarantee that you would find him or her on the same bus looking for you for the rest of the week.

Flirting In Traffic

Sitting in traffic is a great place to flirt. You have all sorts of tools like your side and rear-view mirror. I have heard of many great stories of dates that came about from traffic jams or traffic lights and have even experienced a few fun chat-up sessions myself.

You are stuck there you just have to wait, so you might as well do something productive. It's time to start scoping out the talent around you. If you see someone interesting, make eye contact, then check your mirrors, or check yourself in the mirror, they will really know you are flirting with them then from your preening gestures. When you're done fixing yourself up look back, but make sure you smile this time.

If you want to pursue, just make a fun, funny or sarcastic comment about the traffic situation, or something going on around you that you can both see and appreciate. You could even pay a compliment about their car. If you are getting a good response then you know you could take this conversation anywhere. If you feel like pursing the issue, ask where they are going and then challenge them to a race to their destination. Just kidding around of course! As you can see, the possibilities are endless.

Flirting On An Escalator.

This is a great place to flirt, especially if you are approaching each other from opposite directions. If you are holding onto the center hand rail then your body may already be turned slightly towards the person coming towards you. As you get closer, make eye contact and just as you approach add in a smile. If there is a connection between you, turn your head towards each other as you pass, then turn back to watch each other go off into the distance. But keep smiling.

This is just a very simple interaction between two people that lets each other know you are quite taken by them. If you are getting a favourable response I'd definitely suggest saying something as you pass by.

If no words are exchanged, at this point you have a choice to either glance back at them while giving a gentle wave, catch the escalator going back in the direction your perfect stranger was going, or to just keep on going. If nothing else, it is a great way to enjoy a few moments in the presence of an attractive stranger.

Flirting In An Elevator

Elevators are another great place to flirt. If you are already on the elevator and someone enters, ask which floor they are going to and press the button for them. Smile. If you are going to a different floor, you could always ask them... are you sure you are going to the 14th floor? (or wherever they said they were going) This is a great way to build rapport and have a bit of fun.

If they respond favourably, as you move to leave, you could turn to them and tell them that you enjoyed their company. Then offer your hand and introduce yourself. If you are a guy and you think the woman you are flirting with is flattered and smiling, then instead of shaking her hand, you might want to slowly lift her hand towards your lips, keeping eye contact all the way, and gently kiss the back of her hand. You will make her feel like a princess. And I will guarantee that she will not forget you. It is amazing but it is often these tiny little gestures that get people to fall in love with you.

If you have any questions on how best to flirt in a particular situation, or are looking for tips on how to turn a date into a relationship, please visit www.realrelationshiprevolution.com and send me an email with your question. I will from time to time answer and post some of these questions and answers on this site, and may even include them as part of my monthly newsletters.

And if you have your own great flirting or dating tips that you would like to share. Or if you have experienced a regrettable missed connection with someone who you would love to be able to reconnect with, or would like to reconnect with someone who you have lost touch with please visit www.giveromancea2ndchance.com

Chapter 11

Say What You Mean And Mean What You Say

These days, perhaps more than ever before singles are faced with so many fears and insecurities which revolve around dating and relationships. I'm not necessarily referring to physical safety, but instead, what may be an even bigger barrier may be the emotional security and the ability to trust.

One of the most fundamental ingredients needed to make any relationship work is to have at the core of everything else, an element of trust. Trust is the essential component that needs to be in place for every other part of the relationship to work. Trust is something that is earned and developed over time, but once in place may be the bond that holds a relationship between two people together forever.

In my opinion, the ultimate test of feeling truly secure in a romantic relationship is when we reach that level of trust where we can feel that we can literally put all of our vulnerabilities, emotions and sometimes even our life into our partner's hands. And when we do, we want to know that they are going to treat that privilege with the utmost of care and respect, and that they will protect this part of us no matter what.

This level of trust can only be established over time, and is usually proven by the actions that we demonstrate and not necessarily the words that we say. However, when it comes to meeting new people, building rapport and establishing a bond, we need to prove that we are trustworthy right from the start. And since we usually won't have enough of a history with our new partner to have proven ourselves, one of the ways that we can start to develop this trust is by communicating openly, honestly and congruently.

When we like someone, we ultimately want and hope that the feeling is going to be mutual. But in order for us to find out, we may have to express a little of ourselves first so that the person we are interested in will get the right message. If we are clear about how we feel and what we are thinking we may spark an interest in the person we are attracted to, and in turn hopefully inspire them to reciprocate their feelings as well.

Showing our feelings and intentions doesn't even have to be done by using verbal communication. In fact, our actions, such as how we act around and respond to this person by using body language, facial expressions, playfulness and flirting, may have far more impact than what we say. And, since actions do speak louder than words, we may have to also give up some of our self-sabotaging behaviours that revolve around relationships.

If we, on the other hand are afraid to show how we feel, or if we act in a way that is incongruent to what we say, then the person we are interested in will very likely become confused by the mixed messages we are sending out. They may even interpret this to mean that we are not that genuine or interested after all, and this could be very harmful to the future of any possible relationship.

After this sort of damage has been done it can take an awful lot to prove yourself to show that you are in fact trustworthy. Any mixed messages which are picked up by the receiving partner may also result in them holding back with their own feelings or communication, or shying away altogether.

This expressing of communication and affection, or lack of, which ever the case may be, can be so fundamental in building trust that it is very likely to be the most profound action which will either make or break any romantic relationship at any level.

Unfortunately, whether out of fear or disinterest or for whatever the reason may be, these unclear communication styles are pretty much guaranteed to destroy the potential of so many possible relationships from even getting off the ground. And this failure to express oneself can also prevent a budding relationship from developing into something more, and is often the cause of breakdown in relationships that had previously been successful and happy.

Lack of clarity in communication will also elicit unsure feedback from both parties, meaning that neither gets a clear picture of what the other person really wants. This may well be the reason that so many people walk away from first encounters feeling bewildered and let down.

I have heard so many people comment on this, especially those who have met someone great through an internet date. There is often a huge anticlimactic feeling because even though both people really liked each other and had a great time, neither sent out the right signals to let the other person know. Then, at the end of the date, they walked away from each other not knowing how the other person felt or what they were thinking. And the sad thing is, in most cases they never followed up with each other again after the first date.

For many of these people, at some point, maybe months or even years later when they did happen to run into each other again, and raised the issue of the time that they spent together, they often found out that they both in fact really liked each other. However, since neither one had said anything, and because they were both giving and receiving mixed messages, neither knew that the feelings that they had towards each other were in fact mutual. Even though I believe that it is never too late to reconnect, very often by this time it is just too late because one of the partners may have met someone else.

So as I'm sure you can see, being congruent and expressing yourself and communicating with clarity is of utmost importance when building a romantic, or any sort of profound relationship. Perhaps one of the most obvious things we can do to make someone want to get to know us is to prove that we can be trusted. And we can start to do this by saying what we mean, and meaning what we say.

What Is Dating Anyway?

Besides the issues of mixed messages and the fears around expressing ourselves, one of the reasons that so many people now mistrust each other when first meeting someone that they are attracted too, may very well revolve around the confusion of what dating actually is. And, because they don't know what the other person's beliefs or habits around dating are. This seems to be something that I think has really made a lot of people weary of each other, often causing them to back off altogether.

It seems to me that there appears to be two main definitions of what dating actually is. The first, and I'm in on this one, is that you spend time with someone, either romantically or with the hopes of becoming romantically involved. And, in doing so, even though this would probably start off as somewhat casual, you only spend time with, or date, that one person. This form of dating is aptly meant to be a prelude to a long term relationship.

By putting your attention on only one person it is far more likely that you will both feel comfortable enough with each other to let your guards down and develop the trust needed for each party to allow true feelings to develop. It is also more likely that you will both feel comfortable enough to then start expressing and showing each other how you feel. This would likely never happen if there was a reason to fear that the other person was dating someone else at the same time as seeing you.

To me, focusing on one person is the only way to truly give a relationship a fair chance of developing into something real, romantic and long-term. In some cultures this is, or at least used to be called, "going steady" or courting.

On the other hand! The other concept of dating seems to clash with this idea, and is somewhat vague if you ask me. You date several people all at the same time. The "dates" could be anything from coffee or dinner to any other sort of fun activity, or even casual sex, and there is absolutely no level of commitment or intention to develop any particular sort of committed relationship with the people you are so called "dating." This is fine if you both know what is going on and agree to this arrangement. However, because this is also referred to as dating, it can be misleading to someone who may think there is more to the situation than a brief and casual encounter.

People who prefer the latter form of "dating" are typically serial daters and even though they might say that they want to find that one special person, they are very likely spoiling their own chances of ever meeting "*The One*". Also, when a person thinks, or says that they want one thing (such as a committed relationship) but acts in a way to sabotage themselves from getting it (such as dating several people at the same time) there is a very good chance that they probably have conflicting beliefs about what they really want after all. Or, they could simply be very incongruent.

Their conflicting beliefs could even be that they actually do want to meet the love of their life, get married and settle down. But, at the same time they are trying to portray a certain image, or type of person, that they think other people, usually friends, expect of them.

If someone is aware that they are dating somebody with these particular dating habits, the chances are that they are either going to be very cautious about getting to know them, or they are simply playing the same game. The problem is that when these two interpretations of dating clash with each other, it causes fear in the person who is seeking a soul mate and becomes a major cause of withholding feelings and communication through fear of getting hurt. This in turn may cause so many people to end up avoiding dating all together, because lets face it, they could be setting themselves up for severe disappointment.

This latter form of dating could also be causing a huge breakdown in the possibility of two very compatible people developing a relationship with each other. Because so much of dating and being in a relationship revolves around allowing emotions to develop and having to be vulnerable, this lack of commitment will likely cause insecurity and fear that may lead to at least one of the parties backing right off, even if they were originally interested.

I think that because of these miscommunications and apprehensions about dating, many of us now wonder if a lot of the people we meet (especially online) are in fact genuinely interested in getting to know us. Or, are they just looking for company when it suits them. Let's face it, if a person is genuinely interested in someone they are not going to want to hurt that person or ruin their own chances by dating other people at the same time.

I know that if I am interested enough in someone to go out with them on a date so that we can get to know each other and hopefully find that great chemistry between us, I want to believe that the person I am with is thinking the same way as I am. If I suspect that he is dating other women, then he must have very different intentions to mine. And if this were the case then I'm certainly not going allow myself to develop feelings for this guy as anything more than a friend. I would also probably hold back on giving any signals about being interested in him or about what I want, through fear of putting myself in a very vulnerable situation. The guy will likely pick up on this as if I wasn't interested, and the communication will break down.

I have of course just used an example from a woman's point of view, but I have heard many men express this fear as well.

Not only would I not want to date someone under such circumstances but I wouldn't expect anyone to wait around for me while I ran around town to see if I could find someone better, either. And I certainly wouldn't expect to find them waiting for me when I'd finished with my search. If you allowed someone to do this to you, wouldn't this behaviour mean that you would be the contingency prize? If anything, this behaviour is actually quite disrespectful.

How many people who are genuinely looking for a relationship would actually be interested or willing to do this? Probably not many if they knew what was really going on. And yet there are plenty of men and women who are dating multiple partners in such a manner, and it is enough to put real relationship seekers off by the whole idea of dating, or at least of dating other singles with these habits.

I'm not sure if this form of dating is a sign of the times, a cultural thing, or if it has simply been brought to light by the easy access of meeting so many people through such means as internet introductions. It almost seems that some people use these methods of meeting people as a revolving door where they feel entitled to use lonely singles in what now seems to have become part of our disposable society. But since the term "dating" seems heavily used for both methods, many of us often feel confused about what is actually going on.

Communication is the only way to put both of your minds at rest so that you both know where you stand, so addressing this topic could potentially help put both parties at ease. I think that if we are going to start seeing someone, after perhaps the second or third date, someone should address the question of whether or not the two of you should be, or are, dating other people.

The key here is to know what you want, and what you are willing to put up with, and then to be very clear about communicating it. People don't really want to pry into the other person's life at such an early stage in a relationship, however, I think that it is a question that should be addressed sooner than later. If the question makes your partner uncomfortable or puts them off, then I would be very cautious as the chances are they are not too serious about their intentions with you at all.

Are We Dating, Or Are We Just Hanging Out?

I recently overheard a good looking young man say to his friend, "I'm going out on a date tonight, I think, or perhaps it's just coffee with a friend." "I'm not quite sure."

Hmm... now if he doesn't know if it's a date or not, do you think his "date" will be any the wiser? So at the end of the night when she leans over to give him a friendly hug good bye (because she's not sure if it's a date or not), and whispers "see ya" in his ear, do you think he will be any clearer on the matter? Probably not! He will just have to suffer in silence until he sees her again, then maybe, (and only maybe) he will have the opportunity to figure out if it was in fact a date.

Ever been in this situation? Too many times, I'm sure. I know I have. And unfortunately, although this misunderstanding probably came about because this poor guy didn't want to seem too pushy, she may well be thinking that he is interested in her strictly as a friend. And of course, the same happens in reverse too.

One of the problems I see single people encountering these days is that nobody really knows what the other person is thinking, or what they want from the encounter. If a guy casually asks a woman out, lets say for coffee, but is a bit vague about his intentions, she may wonder if it is supposed to be a date or if they are getting together just as friends. And since she doesn't really know what to expect, it is very likely she will refrain from showing that she is interested in him, if that is the case.

He'll probably pick up on her reservation and interpret it to mean that she just wants to be friends. Then, if both people end up holding back their feelings and come across to each other more "buddy-buddy" than "lovey-dovey" the date could end with two people none the wiser. Buddy-buddy is great if that is what you are, but if you want to develop something more romantic or intimate with someone, you may have to change your ways and your communication styles around that particular person.

This confusion seems to happen a lot, especially when people are already friendly with each other, or when two strangers originally meet through an internet dating site. Even people who are typically very outgoing and chatty and who typically have no problem approaching someone they find attractive, may sometimes run into problems under these circumstances.

You may think that it should be obvious that when someone asks another person out it is meant to be a date, but this is not necessarily always the case. Believe it or not, because it is now common practice to have friends and to socialize with people of the opposite sex, making date plans may not be as clear as they once were. Therefore, unless you are making plans with someone you have already been flirting with, or who you have developed a bit of romantic chemistry with, you may need to clarify your intentions when you ask someone out.

My Experience

After being in a long term relationship and then finding myself single again and out there in the dating world, I soon realized that I wasn't even sure what dating was. In fact, after asking several people what their interpretation of a date was, I found that I got a whole variety of answers. I also soon discovered that some of my male friends, who I may have gone to coffee or dinner with, but where there was absolutely no romantic involvement, considered our spending time together to have been a date.

Being someone who does have male friends, and being a very open and friendly person, I believe that there have been a number of times when I have misinterpreted someone's intentions. If I meet a guy through work or a common interest such as at the gym, and this guy is also very open and friendly and we get along great, (buddy-buddy so to speak), and he says, "Hey lets go for coffee sometime" I think of it as just that-casually going for coffee with a friend. I have later found out, much, much later, that the guy actually thought we were dating. If any of these guys had been a little clearer on their intentions or even altered their behaviour or body language around me, who knows, perhaps some of these outcomes might have turned out very different.

My idea of going on a date, or of dating someone, is spending time with that person on a romantic basis or at least with the intention of getting to know them romantically. Then, if things go well, a relationship will probably evolve over time. To me, simply spending time with someone of the opposite sex does not count as a date. If it did, how would we differentiate between a friend and a date?

If you are just hanging out with someone, going for a coffee or a walk where there appears to be no romantic interest, or at least no indication of romantic interest, does that mean that you are on a date? And, if so, does that mean that you should not be seeing or spending time with other people? Wow-this is so confusing! No wonder we get so bewildered and give off so many mixed signals. This is where casual dates such as going for coffee or a walk can be a little confusing and tend to fizzle out really quickly.

Like many other women, and men too for that matter, if I have any doubts as to the guy's intention or interest in me, the chances are I will file him under the "Let's Be Friends" category and act accordingly. He will probably pick up on my body language and communication style and will get the message, hmmm, she seems to just want to be friends. That could turn out to be an unfortunate misunderstanding.

Knowing your intentions is one thing, communicating them to your potential date is another! If you are going to ask someone out you must be clear about your intentions, and then communicate them clearly. This might seem a little scary but don't you think it would be much easier than going out on a few dates and not having a clue what each other is thinking or wants?

This is perhaps where taking a more formal approach to dating comes in handy. If you want to ask someone out, offering to take that person out to dinner or something a little more formal sends a much clearer message that your intention is to go on a date, than perhaps suggesting going for coffee or a walk would.

If you feel a little shy about being more direct in your communication, my suggestion would be to approach the question in a way that you set the tone right from the start. Try saying something like, "I'd really like to get to know you; I'd love to take you out for a coffee or a drink or dinner, whatever the case might be." If the person you are asking out shows interest, let them know that you will call them to firm up the plans. Then make sure that you take care of the details and call them within the next twenty four to forty eight hours, max!

If you want to ask someone out, you have to know what your intentions are, you need to communicate those intentions and you definitely have to follow through.

Being clear about and stating your intentions will not only let the person know that you are interested but will probably also elicit the feedback you need in order to know if they are also attracted to you. Knowing this may well alleviate the potential for any confusion or embarrassment to either party later on. Also, this allows you and your date to psych yourselves up as you both have something to look forward to. Then, instead of spending your time together trying to figure out what the other person is thinking, you can relax and enjoy each other's company.

If you want some great first date ideas, chat up lines, or flirting tips you will find them on the websites www.realrelationshiprevolution.com

Mean What You Say

There is nothing more disappointing than someone who "talks the talk" but doesn't "walk the walk." You know the type, they say nice things or tell you what they think you want to hear, but they don't mean a word they say. Like people you haven't seen in a while and run into on the street. They make such a fuss over you and insist you have to see more of each other and must get together soon. But, when you respond with, yes sounds great, when's a good time for you? They get a completely blank look on their face because not only did you catch them off guard with your response, but they really didn't mean a word they said. Don't you just love those people?

And then of course we have these lovely people in the world of dating. The ones who agree to go out with you but then never answer their phone or won't return your calls. I hear guys complain of this one all the time. Or what about the ones who ask you out on a date, and when you decline respond by pursuing you like you've never been pursued before. Then when you finally agree to give them a chance, and plan a date, they either don't call to set up the time, they cancel, or they simply don't show up at all.

For some reason, a lot of people believe that they are being nice by saying something that they think you want to hear, but when you think about it, there really isn't anything nice about it all. If people aren't genuine and they don't follow through, it is simply downright rude and disappointing.

If you are going to go through all of the trouble to ask someone out and get their acceptance, you have done the hardest part. If at that point, for whatever reason, you don't follow through, then not only are you letting the other person down but you are also letting yourself down to. You are reinforcing the fact that you don't follow through for yourself, and will only make it harder for you in the future.

Always, Always Follow Through

So let's say that you made your first connection, popped the question and got a phone number, or just made a suggestion to go out sometime. You need to follow through. If you let too much time elapse, for whatever reason, the person that you are pursuing will likely start to get nervous or a little suspicious and may lose interest or create a barrier to protect them self from getting hurt.

Don't play stupid games. If you really like the person and want to go out with them, I suggest that you follow up within twenty four to forty eight hours max, even if it is just to say hello. This will show them that you are genuinely interested and have some integrity.

Also, I'd suggest that you get thinking about where that first date will be. Take the initiative to plan something and then call to let your date know what you will be doing or at least what to wear. This will really reassure them that you are genuinely interested and that you are the type of person who is keen and takes initiative. They will soon get the message that this date is genuinely important to you, and while your actions will make them feel special, you will also be creating a sense of excitement. This is what going out on a date should really be all about. And you can bet that he or she will really be looking forward to seeing you.

There is nothing more flattering than someone who makes an effort to impress you. We all love it when someone finds us important enough to go to great lengths to make us feel special. Remember my point about what makes a person really attractive, it is how they make us feel when we are with them. And if you are going to go to all this effort to make special plans, you will definitely be building up the Brownie points as you are actually giving your date something to look forward to, and a taste of how they can expect to be treated by you in the future.

Don't waste time or play head games. There is nothing more frustrating than being pursued by someone who doesn't follow through. If the person pursuing you starts out wishy-washy with their plans and commitments I personally wouldn't expect much from them anyway, and would likely write them off from the get go. But if someone goes out of their way to put themselves out there initially and then fails to follow through… they will just as quickly becomes toast, in my book. I have heard the same complaints from men and women of all ages. If you are serious about dating you have to make the effort, as it is the little things that separate you from the time-wasters.

If on the other hand you have taken the initiative to meet someone and made the connection but they are giving you the run around, I suggest that you don't buy into their excuses and move on. You have too much to offer to allow yourself to get messed around.

Assuming all goes well (and I'm sure that it will) and you have set up a date, you will then need to decide if you are going to meet at the place you are going to, or if you are going to meet ahead of time and then go together.

Traditional ideas of dating usually have the man picking the woman up at her home, driving her to the restaurant (or other date spot), and driving her home again at the end of the date. Although many women are cautious these days, depending on how well you know each other and what background you have on each other, you may feel that it is appropriate to meet at one of your places of residence and go out together. Whatever your decision, be sure to exercise caution. If you believe the encounter to be safe, many women still prefer to be picked up by their date so that they can arrive together at the destination and then leave together at the end of the date. Ask what is appropriate. I think you're ready, so get out there and have fun. Happy Dating!

Chapter 12

How To Turn That First Glance Into A Date

If after reading thus far, you are thinking that this all sounds a bit scary and that internet dating seems much less of a risk, then I want you to consider this. Not only is internet dating a completely different kettle of fish when it comes to making that first connection with someone, but the actual real life meeting can, and often is a very different experience as well.

Not only that, but if the statistics advertised by some dating sites has led you to believe that the chance of meeting someone online seems more likely than through a natural encounter. You will have to consider the fact that you may well end up playing more of a numbers game. Keep in mind as well that while some sites promote the idea that 1 in 5 relationships now start online, in reality this is only equivalent to 20%. What this must then mean is that the other 80% of relationships are being initiated by some other means, such as a natural or chance encounter.

These statistics then support my own research which showed that most people, when asked if they had a preference to meeting someone through a chance encounter as opposed to an internet dating site. Most responded by saying that they would much rather meet someone through a more natural or organic way, such as a chance encounter or by being introduced to someone by a friend. This was especially true for anyone hoping to connect with someone for a real, romantic or serious relationship, or for the hopes of getting married.

Furthermore, many people denied and still do deny ever having used an internet dating site, and of those who openly frequent them many say that they do so purely for entertainment. Some also claim that they use these sites strictly for the purpose of very casual dating, or to simply hook up for sex, but look elsewhere in hopes of meeting someone for what they call a quality relationship. And while speaking to those who openly admit to using internet dating sites, I have been surprised to find how many still have active profiles after getting involved in what they consider to be a committed relationship.

So while there are success stories with internet dating, it is without a doubt a very different process to meeting someone through a chance encounter. For instance, if you were to strike up a conversation with a stranger, let's say while waiting for your latte at Starbucks. It is likely that at some point during that conversation you will begin to form an opinion about this person. This opinion may be positive or it may be negative, and even though we may do this on an unconscious level, we all do it with everyone we meet.

Not only that, but our opinion will also be based on a very real and sensory experience. And will be influenced by a whole slew of factors such as eye contact, body language, energy levels, facial expressions, mannerisms, voice tone and tempo, sense of humour, and how that person responds to us and we to them. We notice how this encounter *feels* within our bodies. This is a mind body experience which includes an intuitive aspect, and may even ignite that "spark" or chemistry or energy thing that most of us are searching for. A chance encounter will often ignite a *feeling!*

When meeting someone online we often form opinions about people based on superficial things such as their photo and a written profile which may or may not be true. We miss out on the opportunity to experience all of that other good stuff. Then if we like what we have seen we tend to create our own image in our mind of who we think this person really is. If we are not careful we may even fall in love with the idea of who we think they are. This experience is based primarily on what we are *thinking* as opposed to *feeling*, and whether or not we think they fit our criteria.

The unfortunate thing about this is that we can miss out on meeting some great people because they didn't fit our criteria based on their profile. Or, we may become very disappointed with someone who looks great online, but whose energy level or personality falls short, compared to the image of them which we conjured up in our own mind.

Also, whenever a chance encounter leads to a date we go out on that date already knowing that we like each other. This will likely mean that we will feel less guarded, and act more appropriately in a romantic situation, compared to when we meet someone whom we originally met online. This is why you should never put all your eggs in one basket. And in this case I mean, do not rely solely on meeting someone online. With that said let's recap on How To Turn That First Glance Into A Date.

Put Yourself Out There… NOW!

If you take action and practice the skills I've outlined in the book, you will build the confidence you need and want, to start making connections and developing relationships in any and every area of your life. What this means is that you have to start putting yourself out there every single day, and putting these skills to good use. And, you need to start doing it NOW!

One of the biggest mistakes so many of us make in our lives is when we think that we have to wait until we are good enough (according to someone else's standards) before we can have what we really want out of life. And there is nowhere that this is more evident than in the world of relationships.

For many years, women, especially in Western based cultures have been pressured into looking a certain way. We have been told that we need to be slim enough, pretty enough and sexy enough in order to find, and perhaps more importantly, to *keep* a man interested in us.

Men on the other hand have been shamed into believing that they need to be smart enough, rich enough and powerful enough to attract, and keep a woman in his life. And although these pressures now cross both genders, they are lies that we hear and read about every day. And while there are those who may expect a partner to fit into these types of criteria, there are also so many more people who are looking for true love, and who have not bought into this game.

Therefore, I urge you not to make the mistake of thinking that you have to achieve a certain standard, or drastically change something about yourself, or your life before you can feel worthy of finding true love, or having a relationship with a wonderful person. Even if you do want to make some changes, don't hold back from practicing these skills. Empowering yourself in this area of your life may well inspire and motivate you in other areas. If you have some negative or limiting beliefs, or practice these sorts of self sabotaging behaviour then you might want to get some help from a coach.

Believe it or not, not everyone has fallen for these kinds of lies nor does everyone judge you on what you do, or do not have. Love is a very powerful thing, and while there are a lot of people who have been driven by these superficial beliefs, we must remember that this is not the case for everyone.

I know how these sorts of obstacles affect men and women alike, often preventing them from dating or even getting into a relationship with someone who may have even pursued them. Women often have deeply ingrained beliefs that they have to look a certain way, be a certain size, and have a certain look in order to attract a partner. Often thinking they have to lose weight or get into shape before anyone would notice them or possibly be attracted to them.

Although this issue now also affects a lot more men than it used to, they have traditionally been more concerned about not being successful enough. Many men also feel as though women no longer want, or need a man in their lives. And in order to be considered a good catch they need to have a good job, be financially successful, drive a flashy car, have power and status, and own the kind of assets that women typically look for in a man.

I hear about these fears every single day. And yet to be honest with you, most women are far more interested in being with a man who truly wants to spend time with her, than she is about what assets he owns. Sure there are plenty of gold-diggers out there, but who the hell wants to be with someone like that anyway?

The same goes for most men, they would rather be in a safe and comfortable relationships with a trustworthy and loving partner than spending their time with a bar star who may never grow up or settle down. Most men say they would rather be with a woman who appreciates him for who he is and what he does for his partner.

If these sorts of limiting beliefs have held you back in the past then you must start to challenge them now, and get out there anyway. In reality the chances of you running off and marrying the first person you meet is probably very slim, so just get out there and practice. This way you will feel more confident interacting with Mr. or Miss Right when you cross paths with him or her.

Remember to always do whatever it is going to take to feel good about yourself and then get out there and start interacting. A really good way to do this is to become a familiar face. Find a few places that you feel you'd be comfortable spending time in, such as a coffee shop or book store, and start visiting them frequently. Familiarity builds trust.

When out and about be sure to immerse yourself into the environment, be present, be aware of who is around you, be approachable, and be engaging. This means that you must resist the temptation of playing with your phone, texting, browsing the internet, listening to music through headphones or watching videos on your smart device. All of which creates barriers as they tend to give the impression that a person doesn't want to be interrupted, and will more than likely prevent anyone from approaching.

If you are going to read, then read a book as opposed to a digital device. Book readers seem more relaxed and open and less disconnected from their environment than technology users. Also, a book cover with a great title can often be a great conversation starter.

If you are uncomfortable remember to drink water, practice breathing if necessary, or even visualize yourself becoming more comfortable and confident talking to anyone you want to talk to.

Whenever you get the opportunity to make eye contact with someone, or notice someone looking at you, then smile. It is that simple. We have got to get around this issue of avoiding eye contact in order to have a natural encounter. If you haven't already done so, then go back and read what I wrote about eye contact as this could completely change your thoughts around it.

Being a writer I spend countless hours sitting in coffee shops with my laptop. Every weekend I see great looking men pull up outside these coffee shops in their flashy cars or on their motor bikes. They then often sheepishly come inside while looking very uncomfortable to be alone, and seldom do they ever make eye contact with anyone. Instead, they grab their coffee before looking around at the empty chairs, while doing everything they can to avoid making eye contact with anybody who may be sitting close by. Most of the time these guys then go to sit outside alone while still avoiding eye contact with anyone who passes by. If they are lucky, someone (usually another guy) may walk by and ask them about their bike or car. It is only then that you can see how relieved they look to have someone to talk to.

Personally I think this is incredibly sad especially as I grew up in a culture where not only was it completely acceptable to ask if you could share a table with someone, but you'd be invited or included in the conversation that was going on as well.

Now, as long as you are making eye contact and remembering to smile, if the opportunity arises to have a conversation just go with it. Be natural, a conversation is a two way street so it's not your job to keep the other person entertained. If you want to initiate some small talk simply make a pleasant remark or ask a general question and see how the other person responds. It is in your best interest to practice learning how to read people. You might want to observe how people interact with each other and notice what the outcomes are, then pay attention to how others respond to you. This will help you develop some very powerful people skills, as knowing how to read a person and build rapport with them is the foundation for any real relationship.

Practice making eye contact, smiling and chatting to anyone you can. By doing so, you will begin to create the kind of habits that will help you become much more confident and comfortable with the idea of interacting with just about anyone you meet.

Now although the title of the book is How To Turn That First Glance Into A Date, this doesn't necessarily mean that you have to jump at the first opportunity you see someone that you like the look of. While this may be necessary in certain circumstances, it may actually be in your best interest to build rapport with someone first if the circumstances allow. For instance, if that first glance is with someone who works at a place you visit frequently then I'd suggest that you start putting the wheels in motion right away. And you can do so by following the ideas in this book and building a connection with that person before asking them out.

Also, if by chance you do happen to see someone that you really want to ask out, and you think that this may be your one and only opportunity to see this person, then by all means, go for it. Taking this approach is both bold and risky, but sometimes you have to be willing to take that risk. In saying this, walking up to a complete stranger and asking them out will likely catch them off guard, and even if they do like you, they may still turn you down as a knee jerk reaction.

In this case be ready to give them your number or calling card right away and say, if you change your mind I'd love to hear from you. The same goes if you are on the receiving end of being asked out, and you get taken off guard. Just respond by letting that person know that while you appreciate the offer you would like to think about it and get back to him or her.

If you are fortunate enough to meet someone that you like who frequents the same places as you. Let's say, who works in a coffee shop that you go to, works out at your gym, or who catches the same bus as you, then do whatever it takes to make a connection and build rapport. In other words, try to get to know each other a little first so that you can create a level of comfort between the two of you before asking them out.

At the end of the day you have to do whatever you feel will work best for you, but the key to making a real connection is to build trust and a level of comfort between you and whomever it is that you'd like to meet.

When asking someone out, be very clear about your intentions and then be sure to follow through. Follow through for yourself and for the person you are pursuing. Take the initiative, make a plan, set up a great date to impress him or her and give it your best effort. If you say that you are going to call, then call, forget about any bad advice you have ever heard which may suggest messing people around. Honestly, it doesn't work because good relationships are built on trust and respect.

If you say that you are going to call someone to confirm a time and place for the date, follow up with a phone call within twenty four hours, max! Then no matter what you end up doing, give that person your undivided attention. By doing so, you will be using your actions to show them that you are really genuine and interested. Remember, actions speak much louder than words. Good luck on turning that next first glance into a date, and if you need some advice on How To Turn That First Date Into Happily Ever After then check then you might want to check out my new book which is called just that….. How To Turn That First Date Into Happily Ever After

Now I only have one question….What are you waiting for?

Author Biography

Intrigued by the stories of how so many people have difficulty finding the friendship, companionship and love that they hoped to find in their life, Suzanne set out to help singles overcome their loneliness and despair. In the process the author soon became aware of the insurmountable regret suffered by so many men and women that by hesitating, and not approaching an attractive stranger, resulted in a regretful "Missed Connection".

Inspired by these stories, Suzanne developed a workshop and coaching program called, How To Turn That First Glance Into A Date! Suzanne has also now published her first book of the same title.

Let Me Introduce Myself

After working as a stylist, image consultant and coach, I have heard it all. It's true, what people won't tell their hair stylist is nobody's business. I have loved my job as a professional working in a creative industry and meeting all sorts of people, but I have especially loved the fact that I can make people look good and feel better about themselves and their lives.

My satisfaction has not only come from seeing someone loving the way they look when they see themselves in the mirror after I have given them a makeover, but also, through the process of coaching, seeing them experience a sense of joy from achieving something they had previously never thought possible. I love to experience my client's success because this means that I have also succeeded at whatever it was that I had set out to do.

Besides my career in the creative and coaching fields, my real passion and curiosity lies in seeing what makes people tick. I am fascinated by how we relate, communicate, interact with, and respond to each other, and what outcomes result from these interactions. I love to see the shifts that people experience in the process and how change can have such a powerful and positive impact on someone's life as a whole.

My coaching background initially revolved around image consulting, self-esteem and confidence building, three areas that when addressed often leaves the participant experiencing major positive shifts in their lives. The same three areas also very often reveal underlying issues of loneliness and the need to become more resourceful in the area of meeting and building relationships with others.

Being aware of the issues that prevent people from being the best version of themselves possible, combined with my passion to initiate and inspire change, I started out to explore some new avenues and started up a social club for singles. I also become more involved in writing and teaching workshops, writing for and contributing to some local magazines and newspapers, and I subjected myself to the scary task of public speaking. My topics and areas of interest include and revolve around Personal Empowerment, Stress Management, Phobia Treatments, Lifestyle and of course my personal favourite, Relationships.

It is from my learning's, teachings, writings and experience that I have now decided to pull all of my experiences together and write and publish my first book, How To Turn That First Glance Into A Date. It is a powerful book, even if I do say so myself, and I hope you enjoy reading it as much as I have enjoyed the process of writing it. There are several more books in the works as well as some surprise endeavours.

To learn more about my upcoming workshops, presentations, book launches and online programs please visit www.suzanneprice.com where you can download a free coaching tool and get all the latest updates.

Other Books Written By Suzanne Price

How To Turn That First Date Into Happily Ever After

Dating, Relationship or Love – Which One Do You Want – Download the free eBook version from www.suzanneprice.com

It's Your Life So What Are You Going To Do With It?

The Stress & Burnout Awareness & Prevention Guide

Relieve Stress, Anxiety, Burnout, Panic Attacks & Agoraphobia The Same Way I Did

The Student's Stress & Burnout Awareness & Prevention Guide

New Year's Resolutions, Goals, Dreams & Aspirations

I have several other books in the works as well as tons of workshops, presentations and online programs. I'm also developing some apps and an amazing new kind of dating site that you are not going to want to miss. To learn more please visit www.suzanneprice.com.

Suzanne J. Price

Date and Flirt Coach

Life Coach

NLP Master Practitioner

TFT Practitioner - Excellent for overcoming emotional blocks, fears and phobias

Myers Briggs Type Certified in Personality Profiling

Confidence Coach

Image Consultant

British Trained Master Hairstylist

Stress Management Coach & Consultant

Author and Facilitator of Personal and Professional Development Workshops & Webinars

Blogger

Lots More To Come

SJP
Coaching & Consulting~

Offering Personal & Professional Coaching, Consulting & Workshops

Follow me on

Twitter, Linkedin, Facebook
https://www.facebook.com/suzanne.price.395

Google Suzanne Price, Vancouver, Author, Dating, Coaching & Consulting, Human Connections, Talking For Change, Energy Work

And watch out for the release of my new apps

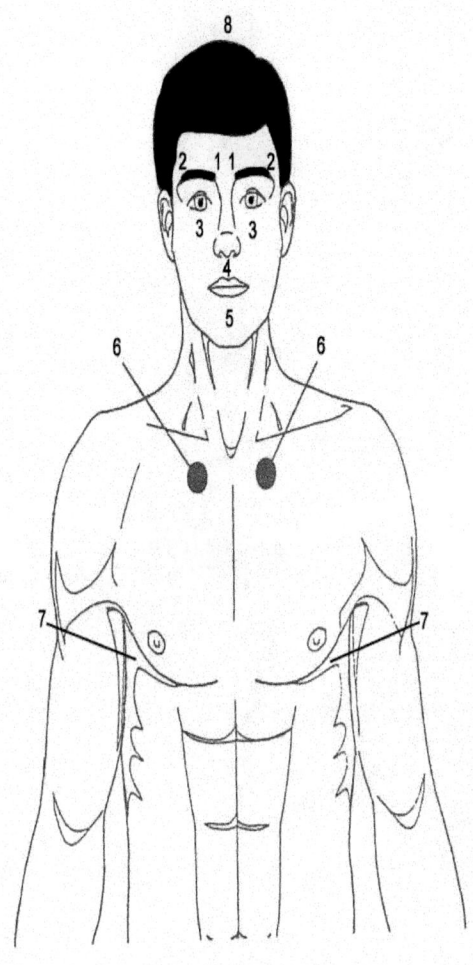

www.ingramcontent.com/pod-product-compliance
Lightning Source LLC
Chambersburg PA
CBHW070737160426
43192CB00009B/1480